The Accountant's Guide to IRS Representation Checklists, Letters, and Forms

2nd Edition

Copyright © 2023 Eric L. Green, TG Publishing

All rights reserved. No part of this publication may be reproduced, distributed, or transmitted in any form or by any means, including photocopying, recording, or other electronic or mechanical methods, without the prior written permission of the publisher, except in the case of brief quotations embodied in critical reviews and certain other non-commercial uses permitted by copyright law. for permission request, right to the publisher, addressed "Attention: Permissions Coordinator," at the address below.

TG Publishing
One Audubon Street, Third Floor
New Haven, CT 06511
(203) 285-8545

Table of Contents

About the Author 8

Why the Practice Guide 10

Audit Reconsideration 11

Cover Letter – Audit Reconsideration 12

Case Analysis Documents 14

IRS Collection Document Checklist - Individual 15

IRS Collection Document Checklist - Business 18

FOIA Request – Admin File for Income Taxes 20

Letter to Client with Analysis – Offer-in-Compromise Analysis 22

Letter to Client with Analysis – No Offer-in-Compromise Due to Ability to Full-Pay ... 25

Letter to Client with Transcript Analysis 28

Collection Appeals 30

Letter with 12153 to RO 31

Letter with 12153 to ACS 33

Letter to Appeals – Withdrawal of the CDP 34

Letter – CAP Appeal to ACS for Default of IA 35

Letter – CAP Appeal to RO for Denial of IA 1 38

Letter – CAP Appeal to RO for Denial of IA 2 41

CAP Letter to Avoid the Filing of the Notice of Lien 43

Response to Appeals Proposed IA 44

Sample Letter – To Collection Appeals Re Follow-Up 1 47

Sample Letter – To Collection Appeals Re Follow-Up 2 49

Letter to Appeals – Response to Collections Investigation 51

Innocent Spouse 52

Conflict Waiver – Represent Both Spouses and Wife Wants Innocent Spouse Relief 53

Innocent Spouse Case Checklist 54

Innocent Spouse Letter – Depression and PTSD 56

Innocent Spouse Letter – Abused Spouse and Hardship 57

Innocent Spouse Letter – Lack of Knowledge 59

Letter – From Intervening Spouse 60

Sample Qualified Offer 62

Letter – Refund Request After Innocent Spouse Relief Granted 63

Installment Agreements 65

Installment Agreements Document Checklist 66

Request for IA – Slight Deviation from Standards 69

Request for IA – With Actual Expenses – 1 Year Rule 71

Request for IA – With Actual Expenses – 6 Year Rule 72

Request for IA – With Step-Up Payment for a Business 73

Request for PPIA – Individual 75

Request for PPIA – Couple 77

Examinations 79

Conflict Waiver Form 80

Taxpayer Interview Questionnaire 81

Response to Examiner IDR 83

Hobby Loss Exam Checklist 86

Hobby Loss Appeal Letter 88

Appeal Letter 1 105

Appeal Letter 2 107

Marketing 110

Marketing Letter – IRS Audits 111

Marketing Letter – IRS Offers-in-Compromise 113

Marketing Letter – Penalty Abatement 114

Marketing Letter – Resolving Back Tax Debts 116

Marketing Letter – Tax Levies 117

Marketing Letter – Tax Liens 118

Sample Blog Entry – Innocent Spouse Treatment by the IRS 120

Sample Blog Entry – Mechanics of a Tax Levy 122

Sample Newsletter 124

Offers-in-Compromise: Doubt-as-to-Collectibility (DATC) 126

IRS Collection Document Checklist - Individual 127

IRS Collection Document Checklist - Business 130

Consult Letter Regarding Offer and Dissipated Asset Issue 132

Cover Letter for Offer – Based on Business Valuation 134

Cover Letter for Offer – Lives with Disabled Girlfriend 136

Cover Letter for Offer – Medical Issues 138

Cover Letter for Offer – Messy Divorce 144

Cover Letter for Offer – Divorce Pending 146

Cover Letter for Offer – Refinanced and Paid IRS Down 148

Cover Letter for Offer – Retired 149

Cover Letter for Offer – Failed Business 150

Response Letter to COIC Analysis 1 151

Response Letter to COIC Analysis 2 154

Response Letter to COIC Analysis 3 156

Letter with Offer Payment 159

Appeal of Denied Offer 1 160

    Appeal of Denied Offer 2 164

    Letter to Town Clerk – With Lien Release and Payment 167

Offers-in-Compromise: Doubt-as-to-Liability (DATL) 168

    FOIA Request – Admin File for Income Taxes 169

    FOIA Request – Trust Fund Liability Assessment 171

    DATL Cover Letter – Counted 1099 Twice 173

    DATL Cover Letter – Challenging a CSED 175

    DATL Cover Letter – Challenging a Trust Fund Liability 177

    Fax Letter – Withdrawal Because They Will Abate 184

Onboarding 185

    Onboarding Workflow 186

    Client Intake Form 187

    Conflict Waiver Form 188

    Retainer Agreement – Hourly 189

    Retainer Agreement – Flat Fee 194

    Retainer Agreement – Consult 197

    Retainer Agreement – Streamlined IA with FTA 198

    Retainer Agreement – Transcript Analysis 199

    Retainer Agreement – Case Analysis 200

    Sample Pricing Structure 201

Other Important Practice Forms 202

    Form 911 – Request for TAS Assistance 203

    FOIA Request – Admin File for Income Taxes 207

    Request for Decertification for Passport Renewal 209

    Power of Attorney – Revoke 210

    Transcript Monitoring Agreement 211

    Tax Information Release 212

Payroll Tax Issues 214

    Payroll Tax Document Checklist 215

    FOIA Request – for Trust Fund Administrative File 218

    Protest of Proposed Trust Fund Assessment 220

    Sample Affidavit 224

    Letter – Voluntary Payment Designated Against the Trust Fund Assessment 225

    Sample Refund Complaint 226

Penalty Abatement 230

    Abatement Request – Bad Accountant 231

    Abatement Request – Medical Issues 235

    Abatement Request – Assorted Issues 238

    Abatement Request – Dementia 241

    Abatement Request – Form 5500 Penalty 242

    Abatement Request – Payroll Company Theft 245

Refund Claims 247

    Cover Letter – Form 843 248

    Appeal for Refund – Past 3 Years 249

Summons Response 252

    Letter to Potential Client About IRS Summons 253

    Letter to Revenue Officer About IRS Summons 255

Tax Levies 256

    Letter to General Contractor – Levy on Subcontractor 257

    Fax to RO – Request Partial Release of Levy 258

Fax to RO – Request Release of Levy of Payroll Account 259

Letter for Release of Levy Due to Hardship 260

Tax Liens 262

Tax Lien Documents Checklist 263

Letter for Discharge – Both Spouses Liable 264

Letter for Discharge – Only One Spouse Liable 266

Letter for Discharge – Carve Out Moving Costs 268

Letter for Lien Subordination 270

Letter for Lien Withdrawal 271

Letter to Town Clerk – With Lien Release and Payment 272

Letter Applying for Certificate of Non-Attachment 273

Uncollectible Status 275

IRS Collection Document Checklist - Individual 276

IRS Collection Document Checklist - Business 279

Uncollectible Status Document Checklist 281

Letter to RO – CNC Status 1 284

Letter to RO – CNC Status 2 – Home Foreclosure 287

Letter to RO – Make Company CNC 289

Letter to ACS – Seasonal Painter 290

Letter to Appeals – Request for CNC 291

Letter for Release of Levy Due to Hardship 294

About the Author

Eric is a managing partner in Green & Sklarz LLC, a boutique tax firm with offices in Connecticut and New York. The focus of Attorney Green's practice is civil and criminal taxpayer representation before the Department of Justice Tax Division, Internal Revenue Service and state Departments of Revenue Services. Eric is a nationally renowned tax expert and author/commentator of IRS civil and criminal tax matters. Having lectured to more than 70,000 practitioners on civil and criminal tax topics, he is one of the nation's best known lecturers in continuing professional tax education. Eric has been recognized by *Connecticut Super Lawyers* in the field of Tax. Attorney Green is a past Chair of the Executive Committee of the Connecticut Bar Association's Tax Section and is a Fellow of the American College of Tax Counsel ("ACTC").

Eric was the 2010 Nolan Fellow of the American Bar Association ("ABA") and has served as Chair of the ABA's Closely Held Businesses Tax Committee.

Attorney Green is a frequent lecturer on tax topics for many national organizations, including Insightful Accountant, CCH, the National Association of Enrolled Agents, the National Association of Tax Professionals, the ABA Tax Section and the Connecticut Society of Certified Public Accountants. Attorney Green has served as adjunct faculty at the University of Connecticut School of Law. He is the author and lecturer of the IRS Representation Certificate Program with the University of Connecticut School of Business. Eric is a contributing columnist for *Bloomberg Tax* and has served as a columnist for CCH's *Journal of Practice & Procedure*. He is the founder of Tax Rep LLC which coaches accountants and attorneys on building their own IRS Representation practices, and is the host of the weekly *Tax Rep Network Podcast*.

Mr. Green is the author of *The Insider's Guide to IRS Offers*, *The Accountant's Guide to IRS Collection*, *The Accountant's Guide to Resolving Tax Debts* and The Accountant's Guide to Resolving Payroll Tax Debts, and the *Tax Rep Guide of Checklists, Letters and*

Forms. He is a contributing author for *Advocating for Low Income Taxpayers: A Clinical Studies Casebook*, 3rd Edition, and has also been quoted in USA Today, Consumer Reports, The Wall Street Journal's Market Watch, TheStreet.com, The Wall Street Journal and CreditCard.com.

Attorney Green is also a member of the Connecticut, Massachusetts and New York Bar Associations, as well as the American Bar Association. Attorney Green is admitted to practice in Massachusetts, New York and Connecticut Superior Courts, the United States Tax Court, The Federal Court of Claims and the Federal District Court for Connecticut. Attorney Green received his Bachelor of Business Administration degree in Accounting with a minor in International Business from Hofstra University and is an honors graduate from New England School of Law. He earned a Master of Laws in Taxation (LL.M.) from Boston University School of Law.

Why the Practice Guide

This guide is a compilation of the documents we use and provide to our staff and to our Tax Rep Members to help them practice. It encompasses everything from our intake documents, retainer agreements and sample letters, to marketing materials to help you attract more clients.

We are asked so often by audiences to share 'our appeal letter' or the 'abatement letter I used to get rid of the $15 million penalty' that it just made sense to compile it all and make it available to attorneys and accountants that can put these things to use in their practice. There are almost 35 million taxpayers in trouble, so the more professionals we can get helping them, the better.

I believe that there are documents here to help every tax pro - from novices to seasoned pros - and it is our biggest hope you find this book enhances your practice, takes some of the mystery out of the voodoo that we do, and increases your bottom line exponentially.

Eric L. Green, Esq.

Audit Reconsideration

Cover Letter – Audit Reconsideration

CERTIFIED MAIL

December 3, 2020

Internal Revenue Service
P.O. Box 9053 Stop 823
Andover, MA 01810-0953

    Re: Audit Reconsideration for TAXPAYERS

Dear Sir or Madam:

We are writing to request audit reconsideration for the above referenced taxpayers for the tax year ended December 31, 2016. Attached is our Form 12661, Disputed Issue Verification.

The taxpayer pays his alimony to his former spouse by having the majority of it taken directly from his pay.

Enclosed are the following items, tabbed for easy reference:

1. Copies of the taxpayer's divorce agreement and its many iterations;
2. A copy of the taxpayers pay stubs for 2016 showing the division of the money between his bank account and his former spouses
3. A copy of the former spouse's cancelled check provided to the company payroll service with the account number to prove the amounts going from the taxpayer's paystubs to his former spouse's bank account
4. The monthly statements of the taxpayer for 2016 showing that the amounts designated to his former spouse did not go into his bank accounts
5. A copy of a cancelled check to the ex-spouse to make up a shortfall in the alimony amount.

In total the taxpayer claimed $29,810 in alimony payments on his 2016 Form 1040. We believe the attached proves he paid $29,800. In alimony to his former spouse and should be allowed the deduction as claimed on his return.

I can be reached directly at (xxx) xxx-xxxx. We look forward to being contacted by you and appreciate your consideration in this matter.

Very truly yours,

TAX PRO NAME

Enclosures
C. TAXPAYER NAME

Case Analysis Documents

IRS Collection Document Checklist - Individual

{Please provide us all that apply}

General:

- Have you filed all your federal tax returns? Yes ☐ No ☐
    - If No, which years remain unfiled?
    - Are the tax returns prepared?
- Have you filed all of your state tax returns? Yes ☐ No ☐
    - If No, which states do you need to file in?
    - What tax years remain to be filed?
    - Are the tax returns prepared?
- Has either the IRS or state taxing authority contacted you? Yes ☐ No ☐
    - If Yes, please provide copies of any correspondence you have received

Assets:

- Do you have a bank account? Yes ☐ No ☐ • If Yes, please provide copies of the bank statements for the last six months of bank statements for all accounts
- Do you own any investments (stocks, bonds, mutual funds, etc.) Yes ☐ No ☐ • Most recent statement for all investment accounts (Stocks, Mutual Funds, Trading Accounts)
- Do you have any retirement accounts (IRA, 401(k), 403(b), etc.)? Yes ☐ No ☐ • Copies of all 401(k) and 403(b) plan documents
    - Statements of value for all other investments, including documentation of loans against any investment
- Do you own any virtual currency, or have you owned any virtual currency in the last 6 years? Yes ☐ No ☐
    - Statement of value of anything you currently own
    - If you previously owned virtual currency and sold it please confirm it was reported on your tax returns that were filed with the IRS. Yes ☐ No ☐
- Do you own or have you owned any foreign assets, trusts, or bank accounts in the last 6 years? Yes ☐ No ☐
    - List any foreign assets currently owned

- o If it includes foreign bank or investment accounts, please provide the last 6 months of statements on all foreign accounts
- o If you sold or transferred the assets, please confirm you reported the assets/transactions on your tax returns? Yes ☐ No ☐
- Life Insurance • Statement showing the premium and cash value of life insurance
- Do you own any real estate? Yes ☐ No ☐ If No go to #8 • Printouts for the value of any real estate owned (appraisal, Zillow, etc.)
  - o Recent mortgage statements for any property owned
  - o Recent statement for credit lines/home equity loans secured by any real estate
- Do you rent your home? Yes ☐ No ☐
  - o Lease agreement
  - o Utility bills
  - o Proof of rental payments for the last 6 months
- Do you own 1 or more automobiles? Yes ☐ No ☐ • Kelly Blue Book printouts for value of each vehicle
  - o Recent monthly statement of any loan balance and monthly payment
  - o Recent monthly statement showing the lease payment and time remaining on the lease
- Do you own any collectables (artwork, jewelry, collections, etc.)? Yes ☐ No ☐ • Statement of value or appraisal for collectables
  - o Copy of your homeowners or renter's insurance including riders.

Income & Expenses:

- We need your current income for you and your spouse/partner/significant other you reside with/anyone who contributes to the household income (whether they are responsible or not). Please get us any of the following if they apply:
  - o A current profit and loss for each business or rental activity
  - o If you or your spouse are wage earners, your three most recent pay stubs
  - o Proof of any social security income
  - o Proof of annuity or retirement income
  - o Proof of any child support or alimony received
  - o Proof of any other income or cash flow stream into the household
- Last three months of utility bills

- Proof of your mortgage payment and balance. If you rent, we need your current lease agreement
- Proof of monthly car payments, whether loan or lease, with the balance remaining
- Proof of health insurance and premium amount
- Proof of life insurance premiums
- Proof of disability insurance premiums
- Proof of any alimony or child support you or your spouse pay, including the divorce or separation agreement and court order
- Home equity statement
- Proof of any judgments and payment plans to secured creditors
- Proof of any payment plans with state taxing authorities
- Proof of student loan balances and payments
- Proof of current estimated tax payments (unless you are a wage earner, in which case they are reflected on your paystubs)
- Proof of out-of-pocket healthcare expenses, IF they exceed $52/per person per month (or $114/month for anyone 65 or older)
- Proof of child/dependent care expense, such as daycare and after-school programs
- Proof of any other necessary expenses, such as mandatory union dues, restitution payments, etc.

IRS Collection Document Checklist - Business

{Please provide us all that apply for EACH business owned}

General:

- Has the business filed all federal tax returns? Yes ☐ No ☐
    - If No, which years remain unfiled?
    - Are the tax returns prepared?
- Has the business filed all of its state tax returns? Yes ☐ No ☐
    - If No, which states do you need to file in?
    - What tax years remain to be filed?
    - Are the tax returns prepared?
- Has either the IRS or state taxing authority contacted the business? Yes ☐ No ☐
    - If Yes, please provide copies of any correspondence you have received

Business Information:

Entity Information

- Name_____
- Address:_____
___
- Federal ID Number_____
- Entity Type (Circle One): Sole Prop / LLC / Partnership / C Corp / S Corp / Trust / Estate
- Does the business have employees?   Yes / No
- If Yes please provide us with copies of the payroll information (number of employees, payroll tax returns and if the company is enrolled in EFTPS)
- Does the business utilize a payment processor, like Paypal, Google, etc include virtual currency)   Yes / No
    - If Yes, list them _____
- Does the business accept Credit Cards?   Yes / No
    - If Yes, provide us the list of cards accepted by the business
- Provide us with the names, addresses and ownership percentage of all the owners and officers of the business

- Does the business utilize a payroll processor? Yes / No
- Is the business a party to a lawsuit? Yes / No
- Has the business ever filed bankruptcy? Yes / No
- Do any related parties owe money to the business? Yes / No
- Have any assets been transferred from the business within the last 10 years for less than fair market value? Yes / No
- Do you anticipate an increase or decrease in income? Yes / No
    - If "Yes" explain why

Assets:

- Cash: please provide the last 6 months of statements for all bank accounts
- Receivables: provide a list of all the amounts owed to the business, by whom, how much and how old the receivable is
- Lines of Credit: Provide statements for all lines of credit
- Real Property: Provide a list of any real property owned, its Fair-Market Value, and provide statements showing the amounts owed and monthly mortgage balances.
- Vehicles: List all of the vehicles owned by the business, including the year, make, model and mileage on the vehicles. Also provide statements for any loans outstanding on the vehicles
- Furniture and Equipment: Provide a listing of all the business equipment owned by the business and any loans against it. If possible, please provide a depreciation schedule if you have one.
- Business Debts: Please provide statements showing any balances due and monthly payment amounts.

Income & Expenses:

- Please provide all of the following reports:
    - A profit and loss year-to-date
    - The tax returns for the last three years (or as many years as you have)
    - A current cash-flow statement, if you have one

FOIA Request – Admin File for Income Taxes

DATE

<u>VIA FAX: 877-891-6035</u>
Internal Revenue Service
GLDS Support Services
Stop 93A
Post Office Box 621506
Atlanta, GA 30362

    Re: Taxpayer:
           Current Address:
           Taxpayer ID No.:

Dear Sir or Madam:

This is a request under the Freedom of Information Act.

1.   Name and Address

    Requestor:

    Clients:

2.   Description of the Requested Records

The undersigned is the representative to _____. We respectfully request copies of the taxpayer's administrative file for tax years _____.

3.   Proof of Identity

As proof of identity, I am including a photocopy of my driver's license and a copy of my Power of Attorney and Declaration of Representative (Form 2848).

4.   Commitment to Pay Any Fees Which May Apply

The undersigned is willing to pay for fees associated with this request. If the request shall exceed $100, the undersigned requests to be notified.

5. Compelling Need for Speedy Response

The Taxpayer is in the process of appealing the imposition of penalties related to the failure to file certain foreign reporting forms and the files are necessary to do so.

I declare that the above stated information is true and accurate to the best of my knowledge under the penalty of perjury.

Please call me with any questions.

Very truly yours,

TAX PRO NAME

Letter to Client with Analysis – Offer-in-Compromise Analysis

DATE

<u>Via Email:</u>
Name
Street Address
City, State and Zip

    Re: **Case Analysis**

Dear Ms. CLIENT:

Thank you for engaging us to assist with tax matters regarding the IRS. As an initial step, we reviewed your case to determine if, with perhaps some planning, we believe an offer in compromise with the IRS is a viable option. In order to qualify for a doubt as to collectability offer with the IRS, you must be able to prove to the government that you cannot full pay your liability (based on certain formulas concerning your excess future income and your net equity in assets) within the time remaining on the collection expiration statute.

Given the current income you are both earning as well as your equity in assets, we do see that an offer in compromise is possible, but would be high, approximately $28,000 for a Lump-Sum Offer, or $49,000 on a Deferred Offer. The formula the IRS uses analyzes both your net equity in assets and your excess future monthly income. Based on what we believe the IRS would view as your excess future monthly income and net equity in assets, we would suggest you consider spending money on some additional expenses that you both need, and that would significantly reduce your future monthly income for the Offer analysis.

We have calculated your excess monthly income to be approximately $1,750/month. In addition to the excess monthly income, the IRS will see net equity in assets of $7,000 from your Ford F150.

Given the numbers we expect the IRS to calculate, we would recommend the Lump-Sum Offer, which would require a check for the $205 application fee and 20% of the

Offer amount to be sent in with the Offer, or $5,600. If the Offer is accepted by the IRS, you would have 5 months from the date of the acceptance letter to pay the balance of $22,400.

There are some expenses we discussed that you should consider that would reduce the Offer calculation:

- Trading in the 8-year old F150 and buying a new vehicle. The loan on the new vehicle you priced out would be $400 per month, which would reduce the Offer by $4,800, and also remove the $7,000 of equity from the F150. This would reduce you Offer in total by $11,800;
- The money you are borrowing to pay us. You explained you need to repay your father for the $5,000. Having a note created that you sign so this money needs to be repaid over 18 months after the Offer is resolved would create a future expense we could claim of $278/month, and reduce the offer by an additional $3,336. Without as note proving it was a loan that needs to be repaid the IRS will not allow this expense.
- You are self-employed yet have no long-term disability insurance to protect your income. It is critical that you protect your source of income for the family, and this would be an allowable expense. The quote you received was $260 per month, which would both protect your income and reduce the Offer by an additional $3,120. If you choose to put this into place, we will need you to have the insurance in force and have made 3 monthly payments before submitting an Offer.

Another critical issue is that for the last several years you have been unable to maintain your tax compliance with your estimated tax payments. In order to do an offer in compromise you must be in tax compliance at the time the offer is filed and maintain tax compliance while the offer pends and for 5 years after the date of IRS acceptance.

In summary, we believe you can do an Offer, and if you implement the suggestions above, we could submit an Offer as low as $9,744. We would need two checks: one for the $205 application fee and another for $1,950, representing 20% of the Offer. Your maintaining compliance is also a must.

Under the terms of our retainer agreement, we have performed the analysis services you have requested. Please call with any questions, and if you wish to retain us to move forward with an Offer.

Very truly yours,

TAX PRO NAME

Letter to Client with Analysis – No Offer-in-Compromise Due to Ability to Full-Pay

DATE

Via Email:
Name
Street Address
City, State and Zip

Re: Case Analysis

Dear Ms. CLIENT:

Thank you for engaging us to assist with tax matters regarding the IRS. As an initial step, we reviewed your case to determine if, with perhaps some planning, we believe an offer in compromise with the IRS may be viable. In order to qualify for a doubt as to collectability offer with the IRS, you must be able to prove to the government that you cannot full pay your liability (based on certain formulas concerning your excess future income and your net equity in assets) within the time remaining on the collection expiration statute.

Given the alimony and rental income as well as your equity in assets, we do not see how an offer in compromise would be possible. The formula the IRS uses analyzes both your net equity in assets and your excess future monthly income. Based on what we believe the IRS would view as your excess future monthly income and net equity in assets, we do not recommend pursuing an offer in compromise at this time.

We have calculated your excess monthly income to be approximately $____/month, which does not include the net rental income of approximately $____-____/month (the reason for the approximation is that it is unclear which expenses related to the rental are already included in your personal housing and utility expenses).

In addition to the excess monthly income, the IRS will see significant net equity in assets. It was unclear to us the exact balance in certain retirement accounts, but given an estimated value of _____ in a 401k (the IRS would determine there is approx. $_____ of net equity in the account), a house with an estimated value of $_____k and a mortgage of $____k (the IRS would determine there is approx. $____k of net equity based on their formula), among other assets, the IRS would expect to be full paid.

If you were to experience a significant drop in income (which you would need to prove to the IRS is indicative of future earnings) or your necessary expenses were to significantly increase, this analysis could certainly be revisited. However, a small variance will not influence our analysis.

Another critical issue is that you are not in tax compliance. Sufficient estimated tax payments need to be made quarterly (based on your 2019 return, it would be $_____/quarterly) and the returns would need to be filed with no balance due. In order to do an offer in compromise (which we do not feel you qualify for), you must be in tax compliance at the time the offer is filed and maintain tax compliance while the offer pends and for 5 years after the date of IRS acceptance. In order to enter into an installment agreement, you must not incur a new tax liability or else you will default on the agreement.

Given the excess income and net equity in assets, we recommend that you make arrangements to pay the IRS in full. If you wish to enter into an installment agreement, the easiest way to accomplish this (without even disclosing financials to the IRS), is to request a full pay installment agreement through Automated Collections Systems (note, a revenue officer cannot be first assigned to your case). You can also request permission to do a "step up"—essentially the first 12 months would be a lower monthly payment (to allow you time to decrease expenses or sort out your cash flow) with the monthly payment increasing thereafter. It is important to note that interest and penalties continue to accrue while in an installment agreement.

It is also our understanding that you are contemplating selling your house. Please be advised that there is likely a Notice of Federal Tax Lien on the property. If you need our assistance working with the IRS lien unit (once you have a buyer/sales contract), please let us know and we can discuss the engagement.

I would also advise having your accountant finalize the preparation of the 2020 tax return as soon as possible. The 2020 return would need to be full paid or the balance would need to be assessed and included in an installment agreement—as mentioned above, you cannot incur a new balance while in an installment agreement.

Under the terms of our retainer agreement, we have performed the services you have requested. Please call with any questions.

Very truly yours,

TAX PRO NAME

Letter to Client with Transcript Analysis

Date

Clients name
Clients address

    RE: Analysis of Internal Revenue Service Account Transcripts

Dear clients name:

You have requested that Green & Sklarz file a power of attorney with the Internal Revenue Service ("IRS") and provide analysis of your transcripts. Enclosed herewith are IRS account transcripts for the years for which you have balances owed: tax years 2010, 2011, 2012, and 2013. As of April 16, 2021, the 2020 Form 1040 has not been filed.

Please note that tax years 2010, 2011 and 2012 have separate assessment transcripts. Therefore, the analysis and estimated collection statute expiration dates ("CSED") relate to you only (the other individual for which you filed a married filed joint return is not included in this analysis).

Information as of IRS Account Transcripts Accessed April 16, 2021

Tax Year	Assessed Balance	Accrued Balance	Estimated CSED [1]
2013	$2,747.26	$2,795.03	3/19/2025
2012	$5,429.50	$5,523.91	9/11/2024
2011	$75,250.78	$76,559.35	10/31/2024
2010	$61,455.02	$62,523.69	5/5/2023 and 7/25/2024
Total	**$144,882.56**	**$147,401.98**	

---

[1] Collection Statute Expiration Dates are estimated and are subject to change based on any subsequent tolling events. It is unclear from the transcripts whether a bankruptcy was filed. If a bankruptcy was filed, the collection statute is tolled for the entire time you are in bankruptcy plus an additional six months.

Based on our review of your transcripts, the IRS appears to have your account coded as "Balance Due Account Currently Not Collectible Not Due to Hardship." This means that, although you will continue to receive Annual Due Reminders and other notices, IRS collections it not presently active on your account (this is subject to change, at the IRS' discretion). This information is based on our best estimation—the only way to confirm if you are in fact in not collectible is to call the IRS (and have someone poking around in your account).

It is important to note that the IRS has filed notice of federal tax liens. It is possible that when the collection statute expiration dates are closer, the IRS may seek to convert their lien to a judgment/foreclose on their lien. If you would like us to perform an offer in compromise analysis or an installment agreement analysis, please let us know. Otherwise, we have completed our work under the terms of the retainer agreement.

Very truly yours,

TAX PRO NAME

Collection Appeals

Letter with 12153 to RO

June 1, 2021

<u>VIA FAX</u>
Department of Treasury
Internal Revenue Service
Attn: REVENUE OFFICER
STREET ADDRESS
CITY, STATE ZIP

Re: TAXPAYER NAMES

Dear Ms. REVENUE OFFICER:

Enclosed is the Taxpayers Form 433 and supporting documentation. Also enclosed is a copy of our Power of Attorney (Form 2848) along with the Form 12153, Request for a Collection Due Process Hearing.

We are proposing a full-pay installment agreement of $1,150 per month. We understand that, based upon the allowable standards you would normally want $1,560 per month, but we believe the taxpayers would be unable to maintain that with their actual expenses, and this payment amount should allow them to maintain tax compliance and repay the IRS within the time remaining on the CSED.

We have included the Form 12153 to protect the taxpayer's CDP and Tax Court rights, though we hope we can resolve this with you in the 45 days that you can hold the case. If this is acceptable, please let us know and we can fax over the 12256 to withdraw the CDP request.

Please call after you have reviewed the package.

Very truly yours,

TAX PRO NAME

C. TAXPAYERS

Letter with 12153 to ACS

June 1, 2021

Internal Revenue Services
P.O. Box 8208
Philadelphia, PA 19101-8208

    Re: **TAXPAYERS (SSNs)**

Dear Sir or Madam:

Enclosed please find Form 12153, our request for a Collection Due Process hearing.

We have checked the box to request the taxpayer be placed in uncollectible status, though we are still working through their financial situation. We will submit the completed Form 433 with documents by the time we hear from a Settlement Officer.

If you have any questions or concerns please feel free to contact me at (203) XXX-XXXX.

Very truly yours,

TAX PRO NAME

Enclosures

C. TAXPAYERS

Letter to Appeals – Withdrawal of the CDP

June 1, 2021

<u>Via Fax: 866-217-8636</u>
Internal Revenue Service
Office of Appeals
SO NAME
Street Address
City, State Zip

Re: TAXPAYER NAMES AND SOCIAL SECURITY NUMBERS

Dear Mr. SETTLEMENT OFFICER:

We have worked out an arrangement with the Revenue Officer and the Taxpayer will be given the Installment Agreement they requested. Please find our Form 12256 withdrawing the Collection Due Process request attached.

Thank you. Please call with any questions.

Very truly yours,

TAX PRO NAME

C. TAXPAYERS

Letter – CAP Appeal to ACS for Default of IA

June 1, 2021

<u>VIA OVERNIGHT MAIL</u>
Department of the Treasury
Internal Revenue Service
Philadelphia, PA 19255-0030

    Re: NAME LLC
           EIN XXXXXXX

Dear Sir or Madam:

Pursuant to Notice CP 523 dated December 13, 2021, the Taxpayer, NAME, LLC ("NAME" or "Taxpayer") disagrees with the IRS' Proposed Intent to Terminate Installment Agreement and hereby submits the enclosed Form 9423, Collection Appeal Request requesting a Collection Appeals Process (CAP) hearing.

Background

The Taxpayer's case was assigned to the field and on or around July 2020, an installment agreement was established to resolve the outstanding tax obligations. The Taxpayer has remained in tax-compliance and current in the installment agreement. There was an issue with the installment agreement—FTD penalties were assessed for periods prior to July 2020 (when the agreement was established). Once the FTD penalties were assessed, they were promptly paid. The original revenue officer, RO NAME, was in a rush to close the case as he was being transferred to IRS Appeals—he is no longer available to assist in this matter. The "new" assessments were fully paid.

Further, when the IRS stopped debiting the bank account, the Taxpayer continued to make his monthly installment agreement payments.

The undersigned has spoken with IRS ACS several times regarding the account. At one point, the IRS ACS even confirmed the Taxpayer was no longer in default status because those payments were made. To date, the Taxpayer has continued to make his regular monthly installment agreement payments and remain in current tax compliance.

During the undersigned's attempts to reinstate the installment agreement (as well as address the IRS' removal of the cross-reference status of the owner, OWNER NAME, due to the issues described above), it was discovered there was another issue regarding a 2017 Form 945 balance.

I. 2017 Form 945 Liabilities

Once undersigned became aware of a secondary issue concerning a Form 945 for 2017, the Taxpayer filed a Form 911 with the IRS Taxpayer Advocate Service ("TAS"). With the assistance of TAS, the undersigned was able to learn a 2017 Form 945 was prepared and signed by the IRS under the Authority of Section 6020(b) of the IRS Code. The Taxpayer recently received a copy of the IRS' Explanation of Proposed Backup Withholding Tax. After much investigation, it appears the Taxpayer's bookkeeper may have mistakenly filed a 2017 Form 1099 without a proper EIN on the form. The most recent update from IRS TAS indicated TAS was that it was "referring the case to a Technical Advisor, as the case is getting more complex than I anticipated. We are working through an unprecedented high inventory levels. Our technical advisors are taking longer than usual to review the cases. I'll contact you again with an update by Mar. 8, 2022." Thus, this issue is being actively addressed and remedied.

The Taxpayer has made every effort to research and resolve these issues and has continued to make the monthly installment agreement payments timely. A default of the installment agreement by the IRS, despite the Taxpayer taking every appropriate action, would be inappropriate.

II. Cross-Reference Issue

When the installment agreement was established, the revenue officer cross-referenced the owner, OWNER NAME's individual account (status 63) so that Mr. OWNER's account would be in abeyance as long as the business's installment agreement remained in good standing. Once the FTD penalties were assessed (on periods prior to the IA), the IRS system removed Mr. OWNER from the cross-reference status and placed him in collections. Now that the liabilities are paid and the IRS will hopefully place the Taxpayer back in good standing, we respectfully request the IRS reinstate the cross-reference status to Mr. OWNER's account.

Request for Resolution

The Taxpayer respectfully requests that the IRS 1) reinstate the installment agreement (including the auto direct debit) and 2) reinstate the cross-reference status to Mr. OWNER. The Taxpayer has proactively worked with the IRS to address these issues timely and has continued to remit the monthly installment agreement payment (despite the IRS no longer direct debiting the payment). The Taxpayer's resources are stretched very thin given the pandemic—the Taxpayer provides in-home support services to elderly and disabled individuals—it would cause significant hardship for the case to go back to the field at this time.

Please process the Taxpayer's request a Collection Appeal Process (CAP) hearing.

Please call with any questions.

Very truly yours,

TAX PRO NAME

C: _____, Case Advocate, Badge # 1000XXXXX, Taxpayer Advocate Service

Letter – CAP Appeal to RO for Denial of IA 1

June 1, 2021

<u>VIA FAX</u>
Department of Treasury
Internal Revenue Service
Attn: REVENUE OFFICER
Street Address
City, State Zip

    Re: **Taxpayer Name, SSN xXXXX**

Dear Ms. REVENUE OFFICER:

Pursuant to Letter 4052 dated DATE, enclosed herewith is Form 9423, Collection Appeal Request requesting a Collection Appeals Process (CAP) hearing.

The Letter 4052 indicates the IRS' "financial review shows there is sufficient equity in assets to partially pay the balance owed." The taxpayer disputes this claim, as the taxpayer has virtually no assets. Therefore, we believe rejection of the proposed installment agreement is inappropriate.

As we indicated in previous correspondence submitted to the IRS, the taxpayer has already liquidated and paid over his IRA to the government. There is a small college savings account that belongs to the taxpayer's daughter. The house located at _____ Lane, Town, State ("_____ House") is owned by Taxpayer's spouse, who is not liable for the tax debt. The apartment located at _____ Street, Town, State ("Apartment") is owned by Mr. Taxpayer's spouse and her sister. The taxpayer has minimal amounts of cash in the bank.

The _____ House was quit claimed by the Taxpayer (the quit claim was executed in 2008 and filed in 2009). All tax debt on any periods owed prior to the quit claim has been fully satisfied. Mr. Taxpayer's wife has her own source of income and she is not responsible for the tax debt. The property was not transferred as part of a fraudulent transfer scheme; it is very common for an attorney to quit claim his house to the spouse due to risk for potential malpractice claim litigation. Mr. Taxpayer has already attempted to obtain a second mortgage on the _____ House but was denied (proof of the denial was faxed on DATE). Even if he was approved for a second mortgage, it is unclear if the spouse would have consented.

Internal Revenue Manual 5.14.1.4(5) states in pertinent part that the government should "explore the possibility of liquidating or borrowing against * * * assets" when considering an installment agreement "unless * * * the asset is necessary for the production of income or the health and welfare of the family." Clearly, the _____ House, a modest house under 2,000 square feet which sits on less than ½ acre, is necessary for the welfare of the family.

The taxpayer has proposed multiples reasonable installment agreements over the course of the IRS collection case in an attempt to resolve this matter. The taxpayer has proposed the agreements in good faith after taking reasonable steps to liquidate or borrow against assets. Due to COVID and the devastating effect it has had on the court system, the taxpayer is in a very precarious financial position. However, the taxpayer is willing to work with the IRS to enter into an installment agreement that is appropriate.

It is our understanding the IRS intends to request counsel's approval to pursue a nominee lien against the _____ House. In a nominee situation, pursuant to IRM 5.17.14.7(4), a separate person or entity "holds specific property for the exclusive use and enjoyment of the taxpayer" (emphasis added). Pursuant to the term table in IRM 5.17.14.1.6, a nominee is defined as "a party having title but not the actual owner." Here, the _____ House has always been in the spouse's name (as a joint and sole owner of the property). The spouse has been an employee of _____ for over 40 years. Her 2019 W2 reports income of $80,394 and her 2020 W2 reports income of $85,639.00. Mrs. Taxpayer has always contributed financially to the household. Based on the facts and circumstances, this is clearly not a nominee situation.

The taxpayer has spent significant time and resources in an attempt to enter into an installment agreement with the Service over the last three years. The taxpayer is exasperated and feels this is a hopeless process. Moreover, this undue delay is placing the taxpayer in a precarious financial position with the accrual of penalties and interest on a daily basis. The goal for the IRS Collection Division is to help taxpayers resolve their issues, not punish them or frustrate their attempts. Yet this case seems to have been nothing but a strange attempt to penalize the taxpayer because he had some past tax issues and is now, in a diligent and good faith manner, trying to resolve them. The taxpayer respectfully requests that the IRS allow him to enter into an installment agreement and close his case.

Please process the taxpayer's request a Collection Appeal Process (CAP) hearing.

Very truly yours,

TAX PRO NAME

Letter – CAP Appeal to RO for Denial of IA 2

June 1, 2021

<u>VIA FAX</u>
Department of Treasury
Internal Revenue Service
Attn: REVENUE OFFICER
STREET ADDRESS
City, State Zip

    Re: **TAXPAYER NAMES**

Dear Ms. REVENUE OFFICER:

Pursuant to Letter 4052, enclosed herewith is Form 9423, Collection Appeal Request requesting a Collection Appeals Process (CAP) hearing. The IRS Letter 4052 indicated the proposed installment agreement would be rejected due to the stated reason that "there is sufficient cash or equity in assets to fully or partially pay the balance owed." The letter also stated all required tax deposits have not been made.

Since the issuance of the letter, the taxpayer has aggressively pursued applying to various lenders for a mortgage on his residence. The taxpayer needed to wait until his 2019 tax returns were complete in order to provide this income information to the lenders. The taxpayer timely completed/filed his 2019 return and has several pending mortgage applications.

Enclosed please find a rejection letter from Quicken Loans/Rocket Mortgage as evidence the taxpayer is pursuing this avenue. The taxpayer has other applications pending which he is hopeful will be approved to will allow him to take a mortgage out on the home.

It is clear that COVID has had a direct impact on his ability to borrow, as his income is significantly down year to date, from the prior year. Accordingly, he will likely still need to enter into an installment agreement for the balance owed. Further, enclosed please refer to an email from a second prospect, NAME of Loan Company, who indicated that the taxpayer "would not have sufficient equity in your home to refinance and cash out the $350,000 needed. At this time, we are limited to 80% loan to value for our cash out refinances." Therefore, the installment the taxpayer proposed in March 2020 was appropriate and should remain pending.

The taxpayer has made his 2020 estimated tax payments (based on his current YTD income); proof of the payment is enclosed herewith.

Ultimately, the taxpayer respectfully requests an additional 60 days to allow his pending mortgage applications to be disposed of. He prays he will be approved, which will allow him to pay down as much of his tax debt as possible. It would be inappropriate to levy a taxpayer who is trying to resolve his tax debt by borrowing from assets. Accordingly, we believe the case should remain coded as a pending installment agreement.

Please call with any questions.

Very truly yours,

TAX PRO NAME

CAP Letter to Avoid the Filing of the Notice of Lien

May 27, 2021

VIA FAX
Revenue Officer
Internal Revenue Service
Address

Re: Taxpayer

Dear Revenue Officer:

Our office is counsel to the above-referenced taxpayers, Taxpayer Name. The taxpayers are respectfully requesting the IRS to <u>not</u> file a Notice of Federal Tax Lien on the real property located at Address ("Address Name" or "Property").

As explained in greater detail in the annexed letter from Attorney (Attorney Name), the taxpayers' interest in Address Name is nil, as the property is significantly underwater due to the primary mortgage holder and other senior creditors' judgment liens. The negotiations with the bank to resolve the outstanding mortgage obligations are precarious and contingent on a quick "flip" of the Property once title is passed to the third party. If the IRS were to file its tax lien on the Property and delay the sale, it will cause irreparable harm to all parties involved.

Ultimately, it will redound to the benefit of both the taxpayers and the government to allow the taxpayers to close on the Property quickly and resolve the debt issues with the creditors that are ahead of the IRS. If this workout arrangement were to fail, the Property would be foreclosed. This arrangement will further allow the taxpayers to focus their energy and resources on paying off the Service as well as retain the critical relationship with the bank, which greatly improves future borrowing capacity and will hopefully allow them to full pay the Service in a more expeditious manner.

Should you have any questions, please contact me.

Very truly yours,

Tax Rep Name

Response to Appeals Proposed IA

June 29, 2016

VIA FAX
Appeals Officer
Internal Revenue Services
Address

Re: **Taxpayer – Installment Agreement**

Dear Appeals Officer:

We are in receipt of your proposed installment agreement of $2,879/month payment starting on July 28, 2016, which would increase on July 28, 2017 by $2,500, for a total of $5,379/month. However, after further review of the taxpayer's current financial situation, we respectfully request that she be allowed to pay $25/month until January 2017, at which time her installment agreement would increase to $2,300/month (and then further increase by $2,500 to $4,800 in July 2017), which would take into consideration the additional circumstances outlined below.

Our request for a temporary minimum payment is based on the following:

1. **Medical Expenses:**

In addition to the sleeping medication which we have previously provided substation for, Taxpayer is in urgent need of orthodontia work that will cost over $9,000. The alignment of her back and jaw were impacted from the powerful intensity of the accident. She has repeatedly sought medical care for both. She has a special regime to mitigate the problems with her back. She is in urgent need of orthodontia to help to address the jaw and teeth alignment as it has gotten worse. We have enclosed a treatment plan from Taxpayer dentist—fees are expected to cost over $9,000. We have added an additional $500/month to Taxpayer out of pocket medical expenses.

2. **Transportation**

We have increased Taxpayer public transportation to $466, to reflect the actual cost of Taxpayer travel to her job in New York City. Please find enclosed the June monthly

Metro North receipt for $366. Also, enclosed is a daily parking ticket for Westport station which is $5.00 if she pays timely. Thus, the monthly amount for parking is approximately $100.00. She drives further to the Westport train station because the nearer station in South Norwalk charges $200 monthly to park and has a waiting list for a permit.

3. Firm Hold Back

Taxpayer firm holds back a portion of her compensation, and pays it the following year. The compensation from 2015 was front loaded – essentially, she received her 2015 hold backs in the first several months of 2016, in which she used to pay her taxes to the IRS, CT, and NY and other necessary expenses. From July to December 2015, her average monthly income is $12,726. She has no cushion to fall back on, as all of her money went to taxes, representation and accounting fees, moving fees to find more affordable rent, and medical bills. Due to the portion of her income that is being held back in 2016, she is essentially uncollectible until January 2017.

Her remaining 2016 income averages to $12,726/month while her necessary expenses exceed $14,000. Her income breakdown is as follows:

Jul-16	$ 19,500
Aug-16	$ 12,000
16-Sep	$ 29,500
16-Oct	$ 12,000
16-Nov	$ 12,000
16-Dec	$ 12,000
Total remaining 2016 payments	$ 97,000
Less out of pocket client expenses	$ (20,640)
6 month total	$ 76,360
Monthly average	$ 12,726.67

We respectfully request a minimal payment of $25 until January 2017, when Taxpayer can get back on her feet. We have explained to the taxpayer the need to budget because her pay varies greatly each month. Moreover, given the additional medical and transportation expense, we request the installment payment be $2,300 from January 2017 until July 2017, at which time it would increase by $2,500 to $4,800.

Please call with any questions.

Very truly yours,

Tax Rep's Name

Sample Letter – To Collection Appeals Re Follow-Up 1

August 24, 2017

<u>**VIA FAX: 855-273-3130**</u>
Settlement Officer
Internal Revenue Service
New Haven Appeals Office
150 Court Street
Room 312
New Haven, CT 06510

Re: Taxpayer; SSN X7420

Ms. Taxpayer; SSN X8660

Dear Ms. SO:

In follow up to your requests concerning the above-referenced taxpayers, we submit the following:

1. **Current profit and loss for Mrs. TAXPAYER:** Please see enclosed.

2. **Face value of the life insurance policies:** The life insurance policies are term; there is no face value.

3. **Status of MS. TAXPAYER's lawsuit regarding her fall:** The lawsuit is still in discovery stage.

4. **Proof of court-ordered payment for Mr. TAXPAYER and when it will end:**
Please see enclosed statement from _____ LLC that includes the payoff, $2,050. We have always enclosed the Small Claims Court Docket.

5. **A statement from the state re: the current balance owed:** Please see enclosed statement, showing the balance owed with the State of Connecticut as $86,974.32. The taxpayers recently defaulted on their payment plan and were required to increase the monthly payment to $700/month. As their account is now with a private debt collector (working on behalf of the state), we were unable to receive a written agreement. Accordingly, we have enclosed an email documenting the agreement. The taxpayers have also entered into an installment agreement with

the Massachusetts Department of Revenue, as they were at risk for levy action. Enclosed please find a copy of the $250/month agreement.

6. **Information regarding Mrs. TAXPAYER's recent health issues:** Mrs. TAXPAYER has been suffering from severe stress attacks and related heart issues. She has been hospitalized and is currently under doctors' care for her condition. Her financial woes have only exasperated her condition. Please see enclosed hospital bills, substantiating a significant increase to the taxpayers' out of pocket medical expenses.

We respectfully request that the taxpayers be placed in currently uncollectible status until their financial situation can improve. We have enclosed updated 433A analysis, showing virtually no excess monthly funds. Further, Mrs. TAXPAYER's business is cyclical, with spring and summer being her busiest period.

Please call with any questions.

Very truly yours,

YOUR NAME

Sample Letter – To Collection Appeals Re Follow-Up 2

May 2, 2017

<u>**VIA FAX: 855-273-3130**</u>
SO
Internal Revenue Service
New Haven Appeals Office
150 Court Street
Room 312
New Haven, CT 06510

Re: TAXPAYER; SSN x7420

MS. TAXPAYER; SSN x8660

Dear Ms. SO:

In follow up to the above-referenced taxpayers' Collection Due Process hearing, we submit the following:

1. **A copy of the 2016 1040 tax return**:
   As you will note, Ms. TAXPAYER's income is significantly down. She had net business income of $9,990. Further, at the insistence of the revenue officer, Mr. TAXPAYER increased his withholding to 22% when their actual tax rate was less than 11% for 2016.

2. **A copy of Mr. TAXPAYER's most recent pay stub:**
   Please find enclosed his paystub dated March 31, 2017. Mr. TAXPAYER is paid monthly and will not receive his April paystub until after our response deadline.

3. **Mrs. TAXPAYER's Year-to-Date Earnings:**
   Please find enclosed Ms. TAXPAYER's commission report. She has had one sale and has earned gross income of $3,663 for the period of January 1, 2017 to April 30, 2017. Her expenses will be markedly similar to her 2016 return, which averaged $577/month. Thus, her net income for a 4-month period is $1,352.34 or $338/month. Due to Mr. TAXPAYER's excess withholding, an estimated tax payment is not required.

4. **Updated Form 433A Income/Expense Analysis:**
   Please see enclosed. As you can see, the taxpayers are still struggling to pay their monthly living expenses. Their situation has further deteriorated due to a deeper drop in Sharon's income (if one compares 2015 to 2016 to 2017 YTD). We respectfully request that the taxpayers be placed in currently uncollectible status until their financial situation can improve.

Please call with any questions.

Very truly yours,

Your Name

Letter to Appeals – Response to Collections Investigation

March 6, 20__

VIA FAX
Settlement Officer
Internal Revenue Service
Office of Appeals

Re: Taxpayer

Dear Settlement Officer:

This office is counsel to the above-referenced taxpayers, Taxpayer Name. In response to the results of the Appeals Referral Investigation (ARI), the taxpayers respectfully provide the following information:

1. **2022 Estimated Tax Payments**

    The taxpayers have confirmed they made adequate estimated tax payments for tax year 2022. In 2021, the taxpayers received one-time gambling income, which they did not have in tax year 2022. Therefore, they paid their estimated tax payments based on the income they received in 2022. While they do not expect to owe for tax year 2022, any balance incurred will be immediately paid, no later than April 17, 2023.

2. **Proposed Installment Agreement**

    The taxpayers respectfully propose to pay $3,400/month in a direct debit installment agreement. It is our understanding that this proposal will full pay the taxpayers' tax liabilities and provide a 6-month buffer for the collection statutes, ensuring all statutes are protected. The taxpayers believe this proposal will allow them to full-pay their liabilities while still maintaining their current and future estimated tax payment obligations.

Please call with any questions.

Very truly yours,

Tax Rep Name

Innocent Spouse

Conflict Waiver – Represent Both Spouses and Wife Wants Innocent Spouse Relief

DATE

<u>Via Email:</u>
Name
Street Address
City, State and Zip

Re: Potential Conflict of Interest and Waiver

Dear Mr. CLIENT and Mrs. CLIENT

We currently are representing both of you before the IRS. Mrs. CLIENT has raised the issue of seeking innocent spouse relief for the joint tax liabilities.

This would normally create a conflict of interest and require us to withdraw from representing either of you and having you both go and seek independent representation. It seems that you are both in agreement on this issue, and so by signing this waiver both of you agree that we can continue representing Mr. CLIENT before the IRS while filing an Innocent Spouse claim on behalf of Mrs. CLIENT to try and clear her of liability.

Mr. CLIENT also agrees that it is not his intent to intervene in Mrs. CLIENT's innocent spouse case to challenge her obtaining relief.

In signing this letter, you are both acknowledging what we stated above is true and you are waiving any conflict of interest. In addition, you also agree that if either of you later changes their mind we will have no choice but to withdraw from representing either of you and you will both need to seek independent representation.

Very truly yours,

TAX PRO NAME

Acknowledged and Consented

_____   _____
Taxpayer Spouse 1   Taxpayer Spouse 2

Innocent Spouse Case Checklist

Potential Client Name _____

1. Was a joint tax return filed? Yes / No

2. Has IRS Collection started: Yes / No

    - IRS off-set the taxpayer's income tax refund;
    - The government has filed a claim in a court proceeding;
    - The filing of a suit by the United States against the taxpayer to collect the joint liability; or
    - The issuance of an IRC § 6330 notice of the IRS's intent to levy and the taxpayer's right to a Collection Due Process (CDP) hearing.

3. Is the joint-tax return valid? Yes / No

    - Did the couple intend to file a joint return?
    - Was their consent by one spouse for the other to file the joint return (express or tacit)?
    - Was the return signed under duress?
    - Was the return signature forged?
    - Is the return unlawful or invalid?

4. If the return was filed without the taxpayer's consent, was their Tacit Consent?

    - Did the requesting spouse have a filing requirement?
    - Did the requesting spouse file a joint return for prior years?
    - Did the requesting spouse participate in preparation of return?
    - Did the requesting spouse receive a tax benefit?
    - Did the requesting spouse have a non-tax reason to file a joint tax return?

5. Is the issue with the return an erroneous item (ie. the income and liability on the return are inaccurate) or is it failure to pay the liability?

    - Erroneous item – IRC § 6015(b), (c) or (f)

- Failure to pay – can only use IRC § 6015(f)

6. Is the couple divorced, or are they legally separated for at least 12 months? Yes / No

    - If yes, look at IRC 6015(c) relief
    - If No, look at IRC 6015(b) or (f) relief

Innocent Spouse Letter – Depression and PTSD

January 27, 2020

<u>Via Federal Express</u>
Internal Revenue Service
7940 Kentucky Drive, Stop 840F
Florence, KY 41042

    Re: **Taxpayer Name, SSN xxxx**

To whom it may concern:

I represent the above-mentioned taxpayer. Enclosed please find form 8857 Request for Innocent Spouse Relief, along with supporting documents. Taxpayer should not be held responsible for unpaid taxes, which are a result of her husbands' business, which she had no involvement with. Her soon to be ex-husband managed all finances for the household.

Taxpayer is a 64-year-old who suffers from severe depression which started in 2013 and was later diagnosed with PTSD. She now takes medications and regularly sees a therapist. She has also been diagnosed with breast cancer. On November 23, 2019 her son passed away suddenly, and she now shares custody of her eleven-year-old grandson. She is currently in the process of a legal separation from her husband. She also has no ability to pay the liabilities and any enforcement will cause a hardship.

If there is anything else, please contact me directly at 203-285-8545.

Very truly yours,

TAX PRO NAME

Innocent Spouse Letter – Abused Spouse and Hardship

January 27, 2020

<u>Via Federal Express</u>
Internal Revenue Service
7940 Kentucky Drive, Stop 840F
Florence, KY 41042

      Re: **Taxpayer Name, SSN xxxx**

To Whom It May Concern,

We are assisting the low-income taxpayer clinic with this case.

Ms. TAXPAYER should not be held responsible for the unpaid taxes. She suffers from both severe ADHD, physical disabilities and has a daughter that is severely autistic and unable to function in a normal school setting.

She also has no ability to repay this, and holding her responsible would simply require an Offer-in-Compromise to resolve, with the IRS receiving approximately $100.00. This would be a waste of the taxpayer's time, our resources (as she is a low-income taxpayer clinic client) and a waste of IRS resources.

Ms. TAXPAYER is now divorced from her abusive husband, but during their marriage in the years in question he was given a separation buyout from his job. As part of their divorce he has admitted that the moneys he received (and caused the tax issue underlying all of this) went into a private investment account that the Taxpayer did not have access to (see attached email), and which he lost in the stock market. Her ex-husband has also admitted in their divorce agreement he filed the joint tax returns without her consent. She had no access to the accounts and had no knowledge the joint returns were filed without her consent, on income she had no knowledge or nor benefited from.

There is also a long history of abuse, and we have several letters detailing this from friends and family that witnessed it. I also have a recording/video of him screaming and slapping her when she had work done to their heating system without his permission.

Admittedly this is difficult to sit and listen to, but I can send you a copy of the video if you believe it would be helpful.

Ms. TAXPAYER is also a perfect candidate for an Offer based on lack of collectability. Her Reasonable Collection Potential is $0.00. She cannot in any way cover her expenses and is reliant on her parents to lend her money every month to pay their bills. Attached to this letter and the Form 8857 are the following documents:

- Draft IRS Form 433
- The Taxpayer's divorce decree
- The email about the private account from her ex-husband
- The list of witnesses that will testify to the abuse
- The Taxpayer's medical diagnosis with ADHD
- Medical documentation regarding her daughter's autism
- A copy of our Form 2848

If there is anything else you need please contact me directly at 203-285-8545.

Very truly yours,

TAX PRO NAME

Innocent Spouse Letter – Lack of Knowledge

January 27, 2020

<u>Via Federal Express</u>
Internal Revenue Service
7940 Kentucky Drive, Stop 840F
Florence, KY 41042

    Re: Taxpayer Name, SSN xxxx

To whom it may concern:

I represent the above-mentioned taxpayer. Enclosed please find form 8857 Request for Innocent Spouse Relief, along with supporting documents. Taxpayer should not be held responsible for unpaid taxes, which are a result of her husbands' business, which she had neither any involvement with nor access to the banking or financial records. Her soon to be ex-husband managed all finances for both his business and the household.

Taxpayer is a 64-year-old who suffers from severe depression which started in 2013 and was later diagnosed with PTSD. She now takes medications and regularly sees a therapist. She has also been diagnosed with breast cancer. On November 23, 2019 her son passed away suddenly, and she now shares custody of her eleven-year-old grandson. She is currently in the process of a legal separation from her husband. She also has no ability to pay the liabilities and any enforcement will cause a hardship.

If there is anything else you need please contact me directly at 203-285-8545.

Very truly yours,

TAX PRO NAME

Letter – From Intervening Spouse

June 1, 2021

<u>Via Fax: 855-277-9041</u>
Internal Revenue Service
Attn. Ms. IRS
7940 Kentucky Drive, Stop 840F
Florence, KY 41042

      Re: Innocent Spouse Claim by NAME

Dear Attorney _____:

We represent Mr. _____, whose former wife referenced above has filed an innocent spouse claim. We appreciate the opportunity to intervene and provide information that you must be made aware of before you decide to provide relief to Ms. _____.

Our client believes that his former spouse should not be granted relief from the joint liabilities because the liabilities were created by her failure to make the estimated tax payments and siphoning off cash from their business. To support this we are providing the following:

- A copy of the bank signature card for the business accounts that reflect that she had signature authority;
- Copies of the bank statements for the years in question that have pictures of the cancelled checks on them showing she signed the checks for the business;
- Emails when she transferred online authority for the Quickbooks file to him that expressly confirm she and she alone had access to the account prior to that (and during the years the liabilities were created); and
- Two text messages from her apologizing for causing this tax problem.

We believe the attached should be helpful in proving that she is not an innocent spouse but rather was intimately involved in the finances of the business and was directly the cause of the tax issue.

If you need any further information please feel free to contact me directly at (203) 285-8545.

Very truly yours,

TAX PRO NAME

Enclosures

C. HUSBAND'S NAME

Sample Qualified Offer

Dear Mr. _____:

This is a Qualified Offer made pursuant to I.R.C. Sec. 7430(g). The taxpayer offers to settle for $_____.00 the proposed responsibility for her _____ federal income tax returns. This Offer shall remain open until the earliest of the date such offer is rejected, the date trial begins, or the 90th day hereafter in accordance with Treas. Reg. Sec. 301.7430-7.

Thank you.

TAX PRO NAME

Letter – Refund Request After Innocent Spouse Relief Granted

June 1, 2021

<u>Via Fax: 855-277-9041</u>
Internal Revenue Service
Attn. Ms. IRS
7940 Kentucky Drive, Stop 840F
Florence, KY 41042

      Re: **Taxpayer, SSN xxxx**
              Reply Reference Number: 0xxxxxxx

Dear Ms. IRS:

Our office represents the above-referend taxpayer, TAXPAYEWR'S NAME. We are in receipt of your Final Determination dated July 29, 2021 concerning the taxpayer's Form 8857 Request for Innocent Spouse Relief for tax years 2008, 2010 and 2011, in which full relief was granted (a copy is enclosed herewith). The taxpayer is extremely grateful to be granted the relief.

Upon receipt of the Final Determination, the undersigned called IRS Automated Collection System ("ACS") to request a refund of the levied payments that were taken from her personal account (see 2010 Form 1040 transcript, code 670 Payment Levy 1040 200712 05-06-2019 -$17,852.16). The levied payment meets the criteria for a refund, as she was granted relief under IRC 6015(f) and the tax was paid within the 2-year period prior to her making the innocent spouse request. IRS ACS indicated that their records state Ms. TAXPAYER is still liable for the entire sum owed on tax years 2008, 2010 and 2011 and that they would not be able to grant a refund due to the outstanding balances.

We respectfully request confirmation that Ms. TYAXPAYER owes no balance for the tax periods in which she was granted full relief under IRC 6015(f) (i.e., tax years 2008,

2010, and 2011) and that she be issued a refund for the $17,852.16 that was levied from her bank account.

If there is anything else you need, please contact me directly at 203-285-8545.

Very truly yours,

TAX PRO NAME

Installment Agreements

5

Installment Agreements Document Checklist

{Please provide us all that apply}

Tax Returns:

- Last three years of tax returns

IRS Notices:

- Copies of any IRS notices, especially if received via certified mail

Assets:

- Bank Accounts
    - Last six months of bank statements for all accounts
- Investments
    - Most recent statement for all investment accounts (Stocks, Mutual Funds, Trading Accounts)
    - Most recent statement for all retirement accounts (IRA, 401(k), 403(b), etc)
    - Copies of all 401(k) and 403(b) plan documents
    - Statements of value for all other investments, including documentation of loans against any investment
- Virtual Currency (Bitcoin)
    - Recent statement of any virtual currency you have, the amount and its current value
- Foreign Assets, trusts or bank accounts
    - Last 6 months of statements on all accounts
- Life Insurance
    - Statement showing the premium and cash value of life insurance
- Real Estate
    - Printouts for the value of any real estate owned (appraisal, Zillow, etc)
    - Recent mortgage statements for any property owned

- Recent statement for credit lines/home equity loans secured by any real estate
- Automobiles
  - Kelly Blue Book printouts for value of each vehicle
  - Recent monthly statement of any loan balance and monthly payment
  - Recent monthly statement showing the lease payment and time remaining on the lease
- Collectables (artwork, jewelry, collections, etc)
  - Statement of value or appraisal for collectables
  - Copy of your homeowners or renter's insurance including riders.

Income & Expenses:

- We need your current income for you and your spouse/partner/significant other you reside with/anyone who contributes to the household income (whether they are responsible or not). Please get us any of the following if they apply:
  - A current profit and loss for each business or rental activity
  - If you or your spouse are wage earners, your three most recent pay stubs
  - Proof of any social security income
  - Proof of annuity or retirement income
  - Proof of any child support or alimony received
  - Proof of any other income or cash flow stream into the household
- Last three months of utility bills
- Proof of your mortgage payment and balance. If you rent, we need your current lease agreement
- Proof of monthly car payments, whether loan or lease, with the balance remaining
- Proof of health insurance and premium amount
- Proof of life insurance premiums
- Proof of disability insurance premiums
- Proof of any alimony or child support you or your spouse pay, including the divorce or separation agreement and court order

- Home equity statement
- Proof of any judgments and payment plans to secured creditors
- Proof of any payment plans with state taxing authorities
- Proof of student loan balances and payments
- Proof of current estimated tax payments (unless you are a wage earner, in which case they are reflected on your paystubs)
- Proof of out-of-pocket healthcare expenses, IF they exceed $52/per person per month (or $114/month for anyone 65 or older)
- Proof of child/dependent care expense, such as daycare and after-school programs
- Proof of any other necessary expenses, such as mandatory union dues, restitution payments, etc.

Request for IA – Slight Deviation from Standards

June 1, 2021

<u>VIA FAX</u>
Department of Treasury
Internal Revenue Service
Attn: REVENUE OFFICER
STREET ADDRESS
CITY, STATE ZIP

      Re: Taxpayer Names

Dear Ms. REVENUE OFFICER:

As you are aware, the taxpayers are attempting to borrow from the equity in their house to pay down their tax debt. We have submitted proof of this on May 11, 2021, and we have enclosed additional verification herewith. There is extreme backlog in the mortgage industry due to the surge in residential real estate and favorable interest rates—the taxpayer is unable to push the bank to process his loan any quicker.

The taxpayers have been desperately trying to address their tax problem. However, given that Mr. TAXPAYER's business deals in commercial real estate sales and transactions, his income has plummeted. Fortunately, things are starting to pick back up again, and his current income shows an ability to repay.

It is our suggestion that the IRS set the taxpayers up on a partial payment installment agreement for $1,500/month (based on his current income). We understand the standards would normally increase this to $2,100 per month, but we believe the taxpayers would be unable to maintain that and remain in compliance. The $1,500 proposed will allow the taxpayer to manage to maintain the tax compliance and repay the tax debt within the time remaining on the CSED.

Please call with any questions.

Very truly yours,

TAX PRO NAME

C. TAXPAYERS

Request for IA – With Actual Expenses – 1 Year Rule

June 1, 2021

<u>VIA FAX</u>
Department of Treasury
Internal Revenue Service
Attn: REVENUE OFFICER
STREET ADDRESS
CITY, STATE ZIP

      Re: Taxpayer Names

Dear Ms. REVENUE OFFICER:

Enclosed please find the Form 433 with all the supporting documents. The taxpayers show an ability to pay based on their allowable expenses of $1,750 per month. We are asking that you allow them to use their actual expenses for 12 months and set up the agreement for $625 per month, pursuant to IRM 5.14.1.4.1.

IRM Section 5.14.1.4.1 allows the IRS to give a taxpayer an installment agreement based on their actual expenses for 12 months to adjust their financial situation to come into line with the IRS expense standards. The taxpayer needs to break their car lease and move into a more cost-effective apartment, which will take some time. By allowing them to use their actual expenses for 12 months allows the taxpayer to make these changes, repay the debt within the CSED, and make it less likely they will default on the agreement and need to come back to collection in the future.

Please call me to discuss this after you have reviewed the enclosed documentation.

Please call with any questions.

Very truly yours,

TAX PRO NAME

C. TAXPAYERS

Request for IA – With Actual Expenses – 6 Year Rule

June 1, 2021

<u>VIA FAX</u>
Department of Treasury
Internal Revenue Service
Attn: REVENUE OFFICER
STREET ADDRESS
CITY, STATE ZIP

    Re: **Taxpayer Names**

Dear Ms. REVENUE OFFICER:

Enclosed please find the Form 433 with all the supporting documents. The taxpayers show an ability to pay based on their allowable expenses of $2,750 per month. We are asking that you allow them to use their actual expenses and set up the agreement for $1,625 per month, pursuant to IRM 5.14.1.4.1.

IRM Section 5.14.1.4.1 allows the IRS to give a taxpayer an installment agreement based on their actual expenses so long as that agreement will full-pay the liability within the 6 years, or the CSED (whichever is shorter) and the expenses are reasonable. This is because it allows the taxpayer to repay while reducing the economic squeeze and making it less likely they will default on the agreement and need to come back to collection in the future.

Please call me to discuss this after you have reviewed the enclosed documentation.

Please call with any questions.

Very truly yours,

TAX PRO NAME

C. TAXPAYERS

Request for IA – With Step-Up Payment for a Business

June 1, 2021

<u>VIA FAX</u>
Department of Treasury
Internal Revenue Service
Attn: REVENUE OFFICER
STREET ADDRESS
CITY, STATE ZIP

      Re: Taxpayer Names

Dear Ms. REVENUE OFFICER:

You should have received a package via Federal Express with the Form 4180s and supporting documentation that you requested. Enclosed please find the following:

1. Form 433B for COMPANY LLC; and

2. Form 433A for OWNER, the company's Owner and CEO;

As you will note from OWNER'S DAD's Form 4180, he retired from the company in 2010. His son, OWNER, controls the company. While DAD remains on the bank signature card, he does not sign checks or have any participation in the company's operations. Revenue Officer NAME previously found DAD not responsible during his investigation in 2016.

The bank statements from 2017 to present that the taxpayer received from his bank do not include copies of the cancelled checks (it would be thousands of pages). The taxpayer can provide a sampling if that is more preferable than issuing a subpoena.

We believe OWNER and the business have the ability to full pay the tax debt. OWNER is currently in the process of trying to refinance his houses in order to pay off, or at least pay down, the trust funds. He anticipates being able to get the balance below $100,000. We respectfully request that you hold off filing any liens against OWNER until he can get approval from his bank for the loan. He has initiated the process and a copy of the letter from his bank is enclosed in the 433A attachments. We were unclear of the value of the two homes and have listed their Zillow value on the Form 433A. OWNER's wages are not paid consistently, so we used the wages on his 2017 W2. The taxpayer expects money will get tighter at the end of the year.

Given the issues that caused the taxpayer to default on its existing installment agreement, including theft loss, a new law regarding mandatory overtime, and a significant drop in revenue from the state, we respectfully request the taxpayer be allowed to enter back into an installment agreement to resolve the liability. It is OWNER's expectation that he will be able to enter into a streamlined installment agreement to resolve the trust fund liability, which would in turn decrease the business's overall liability. We propose letting the business pay $5,000/month under an installment agreement increasing to $10,000/month (the amount of the previous agreement) in March 2019. The reason for this requested "breathing room" is to allow time for NEW COMPANY LLC to begin re-paying its loan from COMPANY LLC to free up additional cash. The taxpayer would like to avoid cutting additional jobs.

Please call with any questions.

Very truly yours,

TAX PRO NAME

C. TAXPAYERS

Request for PPIA – Individual

June 1, 2021

<u>VIA FAX</u>
Department of Treasury
Internal Revenue Service
Attn: REVENUE OFFICER
STREET ADDRESS
CITY, STATE ZIP

      Re: Taxpayer Names

Dear Ms. REVENUE OFFICER:

Enclosed please find a copy of Mr. TAXPAYER's profit and loss for January 2020 to September 2020. As you will note, his net profit for the 9-month period is $22,091.89. Based on the 9-month period, his income averages out to $2,455/month.

With a net business income of $2,455, his allocation of the housing and utility expense is $369 (25%) allocation. Please find enclosed a spreadsheet containing the updated Form 433A analysis. Please note that the taxpayer received Paycheck Protection Program ("PPP") funds in May 2020 of $20,832 (the "PPP Funds"). The PPP Funds were excluded from the taxpayer's gross earnings for the month of May 2020 in the enclosed P&L.

As previously discussed, the pandemic has had a catastrophic effect on the taxpayer's business. The taxpayer is a criminal defense attorney. Courts have postponed or canceled proceedings in response to the spread of coronavirus. It is unclear when Mr. TAXPAYER's business will "get back to normal" in this new normal we are now faced with.

Given the downturn in his business income, the taxpayer respectfully proposes an installment agreement of $300/month. This would be a partial pay installment agreement and the case would come back out for a 2-year review. A 2-year review for this case is appropriate, as the taxpayer prays his income will be back up to pre-COVID levels by that point.

If you need anything else, please let me know.

Very truly yours,

TAX PRO NAME

C. TAXPAYERS

Request for PPIA – Couple

June 1, 2021

<u>VIA FAX</u>
Department of Treasury
Internal Revenue Service
Attn: REVENUE OFFICER
STREET ADDRESS
CITY, STATE ZIP

      Re: Taxpayer Names

Dear Ms. REVENUE OFFICER:

As you are aware, the taxpayers are attempting to borrow from the equity in their house to pay down their tax debt. We have submitted proof of this on May 11, 2021 and have enclosed additional verification herewith. There is extreme backlog in the mortgage industry due to the surge in residential real estate and favorable interest rates—the taxpayer is unable to push the bank to process his loan any quicker.

The taxpayers have been desperately trying to address their tax problem. However, given that Mr. TAXPAYER's business deals in commercial real estate sales and transactions, his income has plummeted. Unfortunately, the market for commercial real estate is not moving. He expects it will snap back as businesses continue to open back up again and return to normal—but there is no guarantee when that may happen. Presently, he can barely pay his necessary expenses. Enclosed please find verification of his year-to-date commissions.

It would be inappropriate to levy struggling taxpayers who are making good faith efforts to resolve their tax matters. The taxpayer plans to retire within the next 1-2 years—although he fears he may be pushed to retire sooner if the market does not turn around quick enough and his employer downsizes its commercial operations.

As the taxpayer has no pension; he is reliant on his retirement accounts to pay his necessary expenses in retirement. Assuming he is approved for the mortgage, he will have an additional long-term expense that he must pay for—he fears if he uses the retirement assets to pay down the IRS as well as gets a mortgage, as soon as he retires (or is pushed out the door), he will have no ability to pay the mortgage. He needs the retirement assets to pay the mortgage as well as his other necessary expenses.

It is our suggestion that the IRS set the taxpayers up on a partial payment installment agreement for $1,000/month (based on his current income) with a one-year review. This will allow the taxpayers the time necessary to sort out the mortgage. The IRS has its liens in place and its interest is protected.

Please call with any questions.

Very truly yours,

TAX PRO NAME

C. TAXPAYERS

Examinations

Conflict Waiver Form

Via Email

July 1, 2021

Client Names
Client Address
City, State and Zip

Re: Potential Conflict of Interest and Waiver

Dear Mr. CLIENT and Mrs. CLIENT

Your tax returns for the year(s) _____ are currently under examination by the Internal Revenue Service ("IRS"). Having reviewed your records and spoken with you we believe there is a chance that the IRS will make adjustments to your tax returns. These adjustments will create tax liabilities that, because you filed joint tax returns, you will both be responsible for jointly and severally.

We spoke with you and explained that the adjustments look like they will be due to _____'s business, and therefore _____ has a potential innocent spouse defense to this liability. This creates a potential conflict of interest for us to continue representing both of you during this audit, and pursuant to our ethics rules, we have recommended to you that _____ seek independent representation in this matter.

In signing this letter, you are acknowledging that we have recommended that _____ seek independent representation, that you have chosen not to seek independent representation, and you are waiving this conflict of interest and want us to continue representing both of you in this matter.

Very truly yours,

TAX PRO NAME
Acknowledged and Consented

_____   _____
Taxpayer Spouse 1   Taxpayer Spouse 2

Taxpayer Interview Questionnaire

- What are your principal products?
- How long have you been in business?
- Who are your principal customers?
- Do you have any other source of income?
- How are sales handled?
- Do you use cash or accrual method?
- How are you recording your numbers?
- If accrual, do you have a list of accounts payable and receivable?
- How are prices set?
- What is your markup percentage? (Ask for markup % on each major product)
- How often is inventory taken, and by whom?
- Who keeps the books?
- Is all income properly reported on the return?
- How did you learn recordkeeping?
- What bank accounts do you have?
- Do you deposit everything? Who makes the deposits?
- How do you get cash to spend?
- Check to cash?
- How are personal withdrawals handled?
- Do you have a safe deposit box?
- How do you record expenses?

- How were the return figures arrived at?
- How are the expenses paid?
- Do you have cash on hand?
- How much?
- Where is it located?
- Do you have nontaxable income such as pensions, loans, gifts, inheritances?
- Do you have investments such as stocks or real estate?
- Do you have any major Expenses such as loan repayments?
- Do you have any asset acquisitions? When? How?
- Have you had any schooling?

Response to Examiner IDR

<u>VIA CERTIFIED MAIL</u>

June 28, 2018

Internal Revenue Service
Attn: EXAMINER NAME
Street Address
City, State Zip

    RE: TAXPAYER NAME, SSN

Dear Mr. AUDITOR:

We have compiled the attached documentation in response to your information requests for the tax years 2014 through 2016. I apologize for the delay in getting this information to you but we had a lot of documentation to sort through and review, so thank you for both extensions.

1.   Medical and Dental Expenses (per Schedule A): Attached are the taxpayers support for their medical and dental expenses. We discovered that in using Turbo Tax the software failed to deduct related insurance company reimbursements despite the fact that they were input as such.

Medical and dental expenses net of insurance reimbursements for these years totaled:

    2014: $13,217

    2015: $10,772

    2016: $ 9,998

See Attachment A for receipt copies for medical and dental expenses not subject to insurance reimbursement and paid for by the taxpayers by check, cash, or credit card. Health insurance payment documentation for these years is also provided.

2.   Unreimbursed Employee Business Expenses (per Schedule A): The only year for which unreimbursed employee business expenses were filed was 2015. These expenses were presented on form 2106 and represented the standard mileage

allowance for miles driven by Mr. TAXPAYER in the course of his business. Mr TAXPAYER's family possessed two vehicles throughout the 2014 - 2016 tax years. One vehicle was utilized for personal purposes, and one vehicle was utilized by Mr. TAXPAYER exclusively for business purposes.

Mr. TAXPAYER works from his home due to the fact that his wife is very ill, and he has an entire home office outfitted for exclusively such purpose. IRS Examiner PRIOR AUDITOR audited Mr. TAXPAYER's 2013 tax return and visited him in his home office and allowed the office as an expense. See the attached Audit report from the 2013 Exam.

The standard mileage allowance was consistently used to determine automobile expenses in connection with Mr. TAXPAYER's business. Miles driven for business purposes were as follows for these years:

2014: 28,066 miles,

2015: 30,773 miles

2016: 30,221 miles

See Attachment B for copies of the mileage logs maintained by Mr. TAXPAYER for each of the three years. In addition, we have provided service receipts from a VALVOLINE Service Center at key dates in 2014 and 2016 which identify the number of miles driven by Mr. TAXPAYER per the readings of the odometer as recorded on each receipt.

A comparison of odometer mileage as recorded on the car service receipts with the mileage readings on the mileage logs maintained by the taxpayer for those dates show that both sets of records are in agreement. Based on accurately maintained mileage logs and service receipts, we conclude that the taxpayers accurately summarized and reported business mileage information for each of the tax years under review.

3. Other Income Per Line 21 Of The 1040: Our review of other income reported on Line 21 of Form 1040 for the tax years under review disclosed only year for which this information was reported. The tax year for which Other Income was reported was 2016

in the amount of $1,723 which resulted from gambling winnings as summarized on 1099 G received by the taxpayers. We are aware of no other instances of Mr. TAXPAYER receiving other income for the years under review.

4. Expenses Under Reported In Error By The Taxpayer: In our review of the taxpayers records, certain allowable expenses were understated with respect to the tax years under review:

    a. Allowable Mileage: For tax year 2014 the mileage driven on the car utilized for business between 1/1/2014 and mid July 2014 (the Trailblazer) was 15,081 (see mileage log per Attachment B. The taxpayer reported only 14,127 miles as driven in this vehicle during that tax year. This resulted in an understatement totaling 954 miles at 54.5 cents per mile for $ 463.

    b. Business Use Of The Home: For tax year 2014 the taxpayer omitted in error the reporting of expenses associated with the business use of his primary residence. These expenses totaled $3,228.

If you have any questions or concerns after you review the enclosed information please do not hesitate to contact me.

Very truly yours,

TAX PRO NAME
Enclosures
C. TAXPAYER

Hobby Loss Exam Checklist

1. Way the Taxpayer Carries on the Activity
   - Separate Entity
   - Separate Bank Accounts
   - Separate Books
   - Accountants and Attorneys Involved
   - Run and managed in a professional manner?
2. The Expertise of the Taxpayer
   - Taxpayer's background in the subject
   - Did they bring in consultants/outside experts?
   - Did they take special training or courses?
3. The Time and Effort Expended in Carrying on the Activity
   - How much time does the activity take?
   - Is it when it suits the taxpayer or at pre-set times?
   - Are these activities fun or are they unpleasant?
4. Expectation that the Assets will Appreciate
   - Are there assets that appreciate as part of the activity?
   - Are the assets used being improved so their value will increase?
5. The Taxpayer's Success in similar Activities
   - Has the taxpayer been involved in similar activities?
   - Has the taxpayer had another business before, and if so was it successful?
6. Taxpayers History of Income or Losses
   - Has the activity had any profits?
   - If the activity has had losses, have they been decreasing over time
   - If there are losses what do the losses look like if depreciation is removed as an expense
7. The Amount of Occasional profits, if Any
   - Does the activity have any history of profits?
   - What is the outlook for the activity to become profitable?

- Are there profits if non-cash expenses are removed (amortization/depreciation)
8. The Financial Status of the Taxpayer
    - Does the activity represent a material investment of the taxpayer's money and time?
    - Is the taxpayer wealthy so that the activity, if lost, would not affect them financially?
9. Elements of Pleasure or Recreation
    - Are the activities undertaken by the taxpayer to manage the business fun or not?
    - Is it the type of activity that someone would do seeking to have fun?

Hobby Loss Appeal Letter

May __, 202__

Internal Revenue Service
Appeals Office
Attn: Appeals Officer's Name
10 Causeway St. Room 493
Boston, MA 02222

Re: TAXPAYER'S NAME (SSN xxx-xx-xxxx); "Hobby losses" under 26 U.S.C. § 183; Tax years 2018-2019.

Dear Ms. APPEALS OFFICER:

This office represents taxpayer TAXPAYER'S NAME ("TAXPAYER") in connection with her appeal of the results of an examination pertaining to tax years 2018-2019. The examiner disallowed certain business losses as so-called "hobby losses" per IRC § 183. We respectfully submit that TAXPAYER was entitled to deduct the full amount of her business losses for the tax years at issue, because she is operating her businesses with the honest expectation of making a profit.

I. General Background

TAXPAYER operates two related businesses, both located at STREET ADDRESS, CITY, STATE. The first is NAME Farm (the "Farm"). The second is the Inn at NAME (the "Inn," and collectively with the Farm, "TWO ENTITIES"). TAXPAYER founded TWO ENTITIES in 2016.

In the northeastern United States, there is significant interest in competitive dog sports, including agility and herding competitions, or "trials." Agility trials require dogs, among other things, to navigate pre-arranged obstacle courses. Specialized facilities with abundant space are necessary in order to train for and conduct agility trials.

As for herding trials, it is commonly known that certain kinds of dogs are bred for herding livestock. Herding trials test how quickly and effectively these dogs are able to "herd" actual livestock within a designated area. Not only must any suitable herding facility feature abundant space and the necessary improvements, but it must also boast actual livestock. Dogs cannot herd ducks and sheep unless ducks and sheep are provided.

There are few facilities in the northeast that are suitable for activities incident to the agility and herding sports. There are commensurately few individuals who are qualified to train dogs to compete in these sports. Accordingly, dog owners often drive for very long distances in order to access capable trainers and proper facilities. Given the distance, these owners must find overnight accommodations for both themselves and their dogs, which most training sites do not feature. This forces the owners to navigate between three different facilities—the training site, a hotel, and a separate overnight kennel for the dogs. This state of affairs has hindered the growth of the agility and herding sports in the northeast.

Before starting TWO ENTITIES, TAXPAYER trained dogs for the herding sports as an avocation. She became quite proficient at it. Given her 25-year background in sports training, animal training, and animal welfare (discussed more fully below), she was able to use this knowledge to develop highly effective training techniques for use on her own dogs. However, over time, she became frustrated at how difficult it was to find suitable facilities. She perceived the need in New England for a singular facility that could provide not only adequate agility and herding facilities, but also on-site lodging for both owners and their dogs. This was the idea that eventually blossomed into TWO ENTITIES.

The Farm provides world-class agility and herding courses, together with actual livestock for the dogs to herd, including ducks and sheep. According to TAXPAYER, the Farm is the only facility in STATE capable of hosting National Specialty Herding Trials for the American Kennel Club, and it does host these and other competitions regularly. The Farm also boasts a first-rate, on-site kennel. This is a tremendous convenience for TAXPAYER's dog-owner clientele who need to stay overnight. The owners themselves can lodge on-site at the Inn, while the dogs can board on-site at the kennel. Everything is conveniently located in one place.

Further, the Inn is an attraction unto itself. It provides generous bed and breakfast accommodations in the "beautiful country setting" of CITY, STATE. It is ideal for tourists who visit the area for various seasonal attractions, such as local fairs.

TAXPAYER timely filed her personal income tax returns for 2018 and 2019. She submitted separate schedules C for the Inn and the Farm, respectively. In 2018, TAXPAYER claimed a net loss of $12,568 for the Inn, and a net loss of $25,190 for the Farm, for a total loss of $37,758. In 2019, TAXPAYER claimed a net loss of $9,393 for the Inn, and a net loss of $31,825 for the Farm, for a total loss of $41,218.

In process of time, TAXPAYER's 2018 and 2019 tax returns came under examination by the Service. The examiner ultimately disallowed all net losses with respect both to the Farm and the Inn, claiming that they were so-called "hobby losses" under IRC § 183. TAXPAYER strongly disagrees with the examiner's findings. Accordingly, she timely filed the necessary paperwork in order to bring this matter before the Office of Appeals.

We respectfully submit that both the Inn and the Farm are activities engaged in for profit, for purposes of the "hobby loss" rules under IRC § 183 and related regulations.

II. General Legal Principles

If a particular activity is "not engaged in for profit," then an individual taxpayer may generally claim no deductions, with respect to the activity, in excess of income generated by the activity. *See* IRC § 183(b). An "activity not engaged in for profit" includes any activity other than either the "carrying on [of] a trade or business" as used in IRC § 162,[2] or activities "for the production or collection of income" or "for the management, conservation, or maintenance of property held for the production of income" under IRC § 212. *See* IRC § 183(c).

More generally, "activities not engaged in for profit" often include activities carried on "primarily as a sport, hobby, or for recreation." *See* 26 C.F.R. § 1.183-2(a). Normally, the taxpayer bears the burden to show that an activity is engaged in for profit. *See Storey v. Comm'r*, T.C. Memo. 2012-115 at p. 20 (2012) (*hereinafter Storey*).

The basic distinction between "activities not engaged in for profit" and other activities hinges on whether the taxpayer pursues the activity for the *primary purpose* of making a profit. *See* 26 C.F.R. § 1.183-2(a). The taxpayer's expectation of profit does not have to be objectively reasonable, but seeing a profit must be the taxpayer's chief subjective motivation in carrying on the activity. *Dennis v. Comm'r*, T.C. Memo. 2010-216 (2010) (*hereinafter Dennis*). While the taxpayer's statement of her own intent is given some weight, what the objective facts logically indicate about the taxpayer's intent is more important to the analysis. *See* 26 C.F.R. § 1.183-2(a).

The income tax regulations set forth nine relevant factors, but they caution that

> In determining whether an activity is engaged in for profit, all facts and circumstances with respect to the activity are to be taken into account. No one factor is determinative.... In addition, it is not intended that only the factors described [in the regulations] are to be taken into account in making the determination, or that a determination is to be made on the basis that the number of factors... indicating a lack of profit objective exceeds the number of factors indicating a profit objective, or vice versa.

26 C.F.R. § 1.183-2(b).

---

[2] In order for the activity to constitute a "trade or business" under 26 U.S.C. § 162, the taxpayer must be "involved in the activity with continuity and regularity." *Comm'r v. Groetzinger*, 480 U.S. 23, 35 (1987). As set forth more fully below, TAXPAYER spends in excess of 65 hours per week working at TWO ENTITIES, in addition to the time she spends at her "day job." Accordingly, this requirement is easily met.

Also, "certain factors may be given more weight than others because they are more meaningfully applied to the facts in [the] case." *Storey*, T.C. Memo. 2012-115 at p. 22. The factors are as follows:

(1). Manner in which the taxpayer carries on the activity.

According to the regulations,

> The fact that the taxpayer carries on the activity in a businesslike manner and maintains complete and accurate books and records may indicate that the activity is engaged in for profit. Similarly, where an activity is carried on in a manner substantially similar to other activities of the same nature which are profitable, a profit motive may be indicated. A change of operating methods, adoption of new techniques or abandonment of unprofitable methods in a manner consistent with an intent to improve profitability may also indicate a profit motive.

26 C.F.R. § 1.183-2(b)(1).

In analyzing this factor, a court will "review a taxpayer's business plan, books and records, abandonment of unprofitable techniques and adaptation of new techniques, and means of advertisement." *Dennis*, T.C. Memo. 2010-216 at p. 17. Indeed, if the facts indicate that the taxpayer has an actual business plan setting forth a coherent scheme for making the business profitable, then the taxpayer may be found to have conducted the activity in a "businesslike manner." *See id.* at pp. 17-18. Additionally, the taxpayer should maintain some sort of accounting system, not only for tax purposes, but also to enable the taxpayer to make informed business decisions. Business and personal funds should not be commingled. *See id.* at pp. 17-20.

We submit that that TAXPAYER has run TWO ENTITIES in a "businesslike manner." Before commencing active operations, she created a well-written and well-reasoned business plan, which is attached hereto. The business plan shows a clear and systematic strategy for making TWO ENTITIES profitable. First, TAXPAYER needed to acquire a large enough property. Second, she needed to improve the property to make it suitable for herding activities. In this regard, TAXPAYER worked with WIFE and HUSBAND NAME, who at the time were the only other trainers anywhere nearby who ran a successful herding center. TAXPAYER also consulted with Carol NAME, the American Kennel Club's Senior Executive Herding Field Representative. Appendices A and B to the business plan (with updates) show the forethought that TAXPAYER devoted to these matters. They neatly summarize the renovations she has made to date in the course of expanding operations at TWO ENTITIES.

Third, TAXPAYER knew from the beginning that it would take some time for her to build a large enough customer base to make TWO ENTITIES self-sustaining. Dog owners who participate in herding sports are usually quite goal-oriented. They would not develop confidence in TAXPAYER until they saw concrete training milestones reached over a period of time. For this reason, TAXPAYER knew from the outset that she would need to supplement business revenues with income from other sources until TWO ENTITIES could become profitable. The annexed letters in support, submitted by people familiar with this type of business, indicate that it very often takes a long time for such a business to become profitable. Meanwhile, the owner must work a second job.

Fourth, the business plan shows that TAXPAYER has devoted considerable thought to a workable pricing model. For example, TAXPAYER researched prevailing room rates for bed-and-breakfast establishments. Appendix C to the business plan, consisting of various flyers promoting TWO ENTITIES, shows how the rates at TWO ENTITIES have increased over time to meet rising costs and inflationary pressures. This, in turn, demonstrates that TAXPAYER is adapting her business practices in order to maximize profitability.

Another measure that TAXPAYER has taken in order to increase profitability is to refinance the mortgage against the property, which has resulted in a substantial interest-rate reduction (from 6.75% to 3.3%) and commensurate cost savings. Additionally, TAXPAYER is taking advantage of a special provision of Massachusetts law relating to land devoted to certain farm use (Mass. Gen. L. Ann. Ch. 61A) in order to save between $2,500-$3,000 per year on her property taxes.

Still another cost-saving measure is TAXPAYER's acquisition of "guard llamas" to protect the livestock on the Farm. At first, TWO ENTITIES suffered substantial monetary losses due to predation of livestock by coyotes and other carnivores. TAXPAYER, through research, discovered that llamas are among the very best guard animals for protecting livestock from predators—generally far better than guard dogs.[3] TAXPAYER accordingly obtained guard llamas for a $200 donation to a New York-based, non-profit animal rescue organization—this price is a "steal" compared to what TAXPAYER would have had to pay in order to purchase llamas at market prices. By purchasing the llamas, TAXPAYER has virtually eliminated her livestock losses due to predation. The purchase of the llamas represents perhaps the best $200 investment TAXPAYER has ever made in the business of TWO ENTITIES.

The annexed document entitled "Future Plans for Growth" illustrates steps TAXPAYER is taking, or that she plans to take in the near future, to expand operations at TWO

---

[3] See attached industry publications regarding the efficacy of llamas as guard animals.

ENTITIES and diversify its revenue sources. Such plans (some of which are already underway) include:

- TAXPAYER is using the ducks and sheep on her farm for purposes other than, and in addition to, their function as herding animals for dog training. She sells duck eggs for $5 per dozen to an ever-expanding customer base. She also sells lambs for $160 per head.
- Increasing the number of annual training clinics from four to between six and eight, and bringing in outside clinicians to handle the additional activity.
- Holding seminars on the psychological aspects of dog training and competition, beginning in 2017. This is an entirely new revenue source.
- Acquiring a judging license from the American Kennel Club, which will enable TAXPAYER both to reap income from judging and to raise the profile of TWO ENTITIES. TAXPAYER has already passed the test that the AKC administers as a prerequisite for a judging license, so there are only a few more steps she needs to take in order to be licensed.
- Building an indoor training facility. Currently, all dog sporting activity at TWO ENTITIES is done outdoors, although herding ducks can be trained in a small space in the loft of the main barn. This makes TWO ENTITIES' business operations largely subject to the weather (especially the cold Massachusetts winters), which necessarily affects profitability. In this regard, TWO ENTITIES provides a unique value proposition to its customers, as it is the only facility of its kind in the region that engages in herding activity in the winter.
- Constructing additional renovations to make TWO ENTITIES suitable for other activities besides the B&B and dog training—such as corporate destination activities, catered events, and suchlike. TAXPAYER is presently consulting with an event planner in preparation for these renovations.
- Building cabins on the property in order to raise TWO ENTITIES' profile as a get-away destination.
- TAXPAYER is presently negotiating with the owner of a contiguous parcel to purchase the parcel. The purchase will enable her to expand TWO ENTITIES, in accordance with her plans for the future growth of the business.

Still another way in which TAXPAYER has run TWO ENTITIES in a "businesslike manner" is to bill for services provided in a meticulous and diligent fashion. The attached invoices show that TAXPAYER keeps track of what she is owed from her various clients, and she bills for it. If an invoice should go unpaid, then TAXPAYER would take appropriate collection action. TAXPAYER is running a business, and she expects to be paid for her services.[4] Moreover, the invoices are to diverse and prestigious clientele—including high-profile outfits like the Briard Club of America and the Collie Club of America. This speaks to the breadth and the status of the customer base that TAXPAYER has developed through her sound business practices.

Next, TAXPAYER is keeping diligent track of income and expenditures—not only for tax purposes, but also so that she can evaluate her cash flow and make adjustments to maximize profitability. For instance, TAXPAYER's diligence in this regard has enabled her to see what a drain her mortgage has been on profitability, which in turn prompted her to refinance at a lower rate—from 6.75% to 3.3%. TAXPAYER's number crunching has also enabled her to ascertain her livestock losses due to predation, which prompted her to acquire the guard llamas.

As for advertising, the TWO ENTITIES Facebook page sees ample activity. It has become a prolific forum for dog enthusiasts to interact with one another, which raises the overall profile of TWO ENTITIES. One of TAXPAYER's clients has gratuitously posted a YouTube video illustrating the kinds of herding lessons TAXPAYER gives.[5] TAXPAYER has also resorted to more traditional forms of advertisement, such as flyers, promotional items bearing the logo of the business (travel mugs, dog bowls, bumper stickers, etc.), pamphlets, brochures, photo books, and suchlike.

Even so, probably the best advertising for TWO ENTITIES has come by way of word of mouth. The community of "dog fancy people" is fairly tight-knit, so TAXPAYER's clients frequently refer their friends to her. Further, given the consistent competitive success of the dogs that TAXPAYER trains, both she and TWO ENTITIES have been mentioned in numerous trade publications, examples of which are attached hereto. In light of all the free publicity that TWO ENTITIES has garnered in this fashion, TAXPAYER has not found it necessary to spend much money on advertising. *Cf. Rozzano v. Commissioner*, T.C. Memo. 2007-177 at *5 (July 3, 2007)(*hereinafter Rozzano*) (fact that taxpayer made "no great effort" to advertise not necessarily "indicative of an absence of profit motive," at least if she can show that a "word of mouth" approach has successfully attracted substantial numbers of clients).

For all these reasons, we submit that TAXPAYER has run TWO ENTITIES in a businesslike manner, so that this crucial factor should be weighed in her favor.

(2). The expertise of the taxpayer or her advisers.

According to the regulations,

---

[4] The attached entry forms, by which dog handlers sign up to participate in competitions and other events at TWO ENTITIES, also show that TAXPAYER runs TWO ENTITIES in a professional manner.

[5] LINK WENT HERE

> Preparation for the activity by extensive study of its accepted business, economic, and scientific practices, or consultation with those who are expert therein, may indicate that the taxpayer has a profit motive where the taxpayer carries on the activity in accordance with such practices. Where a taxpayer has such preparation or procures such expert advice, but does not carry on the activity in accordance with such practices, a lack of intent to derive profit may be indicated unless it appears that the taxpayer is attempting to develop new or superior techniques which may result in profits from the activity.

26 C.F.R. § 1.183-2(b)(2). Unless the taxpayer already has such knowledge, the taxpayer's preparation should include not only acquiring the skills necessary to perform the activity, but the knowledge necessary to perform it profitably. *See Burrus v. Commissioner*, T.C. Memo. 2003-285 at *12 (October 3, 2003)(*hereinafter Burrus*). The taxpayer may need to seek expert advice on this point. *See Dennis*, T.C. Memo. 2010-216 at p. 25.

The attached business plan, together with TAXPAYER's CV (also attached), should clearly demonstrate TAXPAYER's rich expertise in training people and animals. TAXPAYER has worked and taught, quite successfully, for over 25 years in the fields of veterinary medicine, animal welfare, animal training, and sports training. She has done tremendous work in terms of developing policies relating to the care of animals and their use in research. Moreover, TAXPAYER has taught extensively in corporate and academic settings, and she has often spoken at national and international conferences. Presently, TAXPAYER trains staff at the Harvard Medical Center's New England Regional Primate Center to interact in appropriate ways with primates. She is also helping to close this facility down, and to transition staff out of it. TAXPAYER is considered an expert in these fields, and she draws upon her knowledge in order to carry on her work at TWO ENTITIES. *Cf. Rozzano*, T.C. Memo. 2007-177 at *7.

Additionally, as stated above, TAXPAYER has consulted with knowledgeable parties from the beginning HUSBAND AND WIFE. While TAXPAYER did not follow the HUSBAND AND WIFE' business model exactly, she incorporated elements that she thought would be beneficial, and then she added elements of her own design (such as the Inn, the "working farm" experience, and other tweaks) in order to build what she thought was a unique and superior business model. TAXPAYER's instincts were correct in this regard. The annexed letters in support, submitted by "insiders" to the field, indicate that TWO ENTITIES is generally regarded as something distinctive and irreplaceable. The exceptional combination of dog sporting/training site, B&B, kennel, and mini-resort apparently cannot be found anywhere else in the northeast.

Further, TAXPAYER surveyed multiple potential sites before selecting the property where TWO ENTITIES is now situated. In so doing, she did not confine her research to consulting with the HUSBAND AND WIFE. In addition, she performed her own, informal "market study," in which she spoke with potential customers about issues relating to the site. Based on their responses, TAXPAYER determined that she could run TWO ENTITIES profitably at the selected site.

Moreover, TAXPAYER still brings in outside trainers to help her conduct dog sporting events, and to augment her knowledge base. She has trained with respected herding instructors, including both NAMES. She continues to train with NAME. TAXPAYER also attends seminars and subscribes to professional magazines in order to keep her knowledge current. She consults with ANOTHER NAME,[6] in order to supplement her own expertise on the psychological aspects of training. For these reasons, we respectfully submit that this factor ought to be weighed in TAXPAYER's favor.

(3). The time and effort expended by the taxpayer in carrying on the activity.

According to the regulations,

> The fact that the taxpayer devotes much of his [or her] personal time and effort to carrying on an activity, particularly if the activity does not have substantial personal or recreational aspects, may indicate an intention to derive a profit. A taxpayer's withdrawal from another occupation to devote most of his energies to the activity may also be evidence that the activity is engaged in for profit....

26 C.F.R. § 1.183-2(b)(3). A taxpayer may, of course, carry on more than one activity "for profit" at a given time. *See Storey*, T.C. Memo 2012-115 at p. 28 (taxpayer whose primary employment was as attorney could also conduct filmmaking activities on the side "for profit"). We respectfully submit that this factor ought to be weighed in TAXPAYER's favor.

When TAXPAYER started TWO ENTITIES, she worked at least forty hours per week at her day job, but still devoted substantial time to TWO ENTITIES. This sort of dual employment in the early years is typical for persons opening up dog-sporting facilities, since profitability usually takes quite a number of years to achieve.

---

[6] NAME is the creator of "FAMOUS SYSTEM," a system he developed in order to maintain mental focus in competitive and high-pressure situations. He is a highly-regarded expert on the subject.

Even so, TAXPAYER has progressively withdrawn from her successful, 25-year professional career in order to focus on TWO ENTITIES. As of the date of this writing, TAXPAYER devotes roughly 28 hours per week to her W2 job. Contrast this with the roughly 68-70 hours per week that she devotes to TWO ENTITIES, over and above the time devoted to her W2 job. Additionally, TAXPAYER formerly derived sizeable income from speaking engagements on topics relating to animal welfare. Nevertheless, TAXPAYER has given up her lucrative speaking engagements, so that she may devote more time to TWO ENTITIES.

Finally, TAXPAYER recently made the decision to quit her W2 job altogether, as of May 29, 2015, so that she may devote all her time to TWO ENTITIES (subject to the possibility of taking on part-time work as needed in order to supplement her income). Given the high salary that TAXPAYER earns at her W2 job, this is a major step for her. It demonstrates, beyond cavil, TAXPAYER's commitment to building TWO ENTITIES as an independent and self-sustaining going concern.

As for any recreational aspects, TAXPAYER will freely admit that she enjoys working with animals and people. However, TAXPAYER does much of the work at TWO ENTITIES herself, and that work is not easy. The work necessary to maintain the Farm and training facilities, care for the livestock, train the dogs, supervise students, and run the Inn and on-site kennel is onerous, mentally and physically demanding, and time-consuming. *Cf. Rozzano*, T.C. Memo. 2007-177 at *9 (finding horse-farming operation a business, not a hobby, where taxpayer devoted substantial time to performing necessary repairs and upkeep himself, in addition to time devoted to day job); *see also Dennis*, T.C. Memo. 2010-216 at p. 25 (time and labor required for horse farm offset any recreational aspects of activity, notwithstanding fact that taxpayers might have enjoyed working with horses to some extent).

We submit that no sane person would take these kinds of steps for the sake of a mere hobby, without the expectation of profit—certainly no one as savvy as TAXPAYER. Accordingly, this factor should be weighed in her favor.

(4) Expectation that assets used in the activity may appreciate in value.

According to the regulations,

> The term profit encompasses appreciation in the value of assets, such as land, used in the activity. Thus, the taxpayer may intend to derive a profit from the operation of the activity, and may also intend that, even if no profit from current operations is derived, an overall profit will result when appreciation in the value of land used in the activity is realized

since income from the activity together with the appreciation of land will exceed expenses of operation.

26 C.F.R. § 1.183-2(b)(4).

In analyzing this factor, the regulations caution that any farming activity on the land will only be considered the "same activity" as the holding of the land where the income derived from farming (and perhaps other business activities) exceeds deductions other than those attributable to carrying costs associated with the land, such as property taxes and depreciation of improvements. 26 C.F.R. § 1.183-1(d)(1).

TAXPAYER has expended a small fortune from her personal and retirement savings—over $350,000—on various capital acquisitions and improvements for TWO ENTITIES.[7] She did this in order to avoid saddling herself and TWO ENTITIES with excessive debt, which hinders profitability. This is not an insignificant sum for TAXPAYER, as it represents roughly 2-3 years' worth of gross salary for her at her various W2 jobs. Indeed, TAXPAYER's hopes for a secure retirement hinge on the success of TWO ENTITIES. TAXPAYER anticipates that, when she grows too old to manage TWO ENTITIES, she will sell the property and hopefully have sufficient funds to finance her retirement. No rational person would expend such a large portion of her savings for a mere hobby. For these reasons, this factor should be weighed in TAXPAYER's favor.

(5) The success of the taxpayer in carrying on other similar or dissimilar activities.

According to the regulations,

> The fact that the taxpayer has engaged in similar activities in the past and converted them from unprofitable to profitable enterprises may indicate that he is engaged in the present activity for profit, even though the activity is presently unprofitable.

26 C.F.R. § 1.183-2(b)(5). Additionally,

> A taxpayer's successes in other unrelated activities may help to demonstrate that his present objective is profit.... A court can infer that a taxpayer's diligence, initiative, foresight, and other qualities will generally lead to success in other business activities if he has demonstrated those qualities by starting his

---

[7] TAXPAYER presently has $216,661 in her Fidelity retirement account, of which she has earmarked $25,000 for capital improvements in order to facilitate her planned expansion of TWO ENTITIES.

> own business and turning that business into a relatively large and profitable enterprise.

Dennis, 2010-216 T.C. Memo at p. 31.

As discussed above, TAXPAYER's has successfully worked and taught, for over 25 years in the fields of veterinary medicine, animal welfare, animal training, and sports training. She once derived substantial income from speaking engagements. She was proficient at training dogs even before she founded TWO ENTITIES. Accordingly, this factor ought to weigh in TAXPAYER's favor. *Cf. Storey*, T.C. Memo 2012-115 at pp. 29-30 (treating this factor as slightly favoring taxpayer with respect to her film production activities, where, at her "day job," she was a successful attorney who started her own firm and rose to partner at a large firm, and where she attained some artistic success before taking up film production).

(6) and (7) The taxpayer's history of income or losses with respect to the activity/the amount of any occasional profits earned.

Generally, "[a] history of substantial losses may indicate that the taxpayer did not conduct the activity for profit." *Dennis*, 2010-216 T.C. Memo at p. 32. Nevertheless,

> [a] series of losses during the initial or start-up stage of an activity may not necessarily be an indication that the activity is not engaged in for profit. However, where losses continue to be sustained beyond the period which customarily is necessary to bring the operation to profitable status such continued losses, if not explainable, as due to customary business risks or reverses, may be indicative that the activity is not being engaged in for profit. If losses are sustained because of unforeseen or fortuitous circumstances which are beyond the control of the taxpayer, such as drought, disease, fire, theft, weather damages, other involuntary conversions, or depressed market conditions, such losses would not be an indication that the activity is not engaged in for profit....

26 C.F.R. § 1.183-2(b)(6).

Additionally,

> The amount of profits in relation to the amount of losses incurred, and in relation to the amount of the taxpayer's investment and the value of the assets used in the activity,

> may provide useful criteria in determining the taxpayer's intent. An occasional small profit from an activity generating large losses, or from an activity in which the taxpayer has made a large investment, would not generally be determinative that the activity is engaged in for profit. However, substantial profit, though only occasional, would generally be indicative that an activity is engaged in for profit, where the investment or losses are comparatively small.

26 C.F.R. § 1.183-2(b)(7). Generally, the Tax Court will "examine the sixth and seventh factors, the taxpayer's history of income or losses with respect to the activity and amount of any occasional profits, in tandem." *Storey*, T.C. Memo 2012-115 at p. 30.

Here, TWO ENTITIES incurred considerable losses between 2016 (the year of inception) and 2019. However, gross income at TWO ENTITIES is now on a clear upward trajectory. Indeed, as the annexed spreadsheets demonstrate, gross revenues for 2020 increased by roughly 50% from 2019 for both the Inn and the Farm. Specifically, 2019 gross revenue for the Farm was $16,850, but 2020 gross revenue for the Farm was $24,697. Similarly, 2019 gross revenue for the Inn was $6,675, but 2020 gross revenue for the Inn was $9,450. Even in 2019, the Inn posted a tentative profit, before taking into account certain depreciation deductions. (TAXPAYER's recent tax returns are attached).

Additionally, the number of students that TAXPAYER trains has grown from three in the beginning to more than 70 now. TAXPAYER's student and customer bases keeps growing, right along with her revenue. Her determination and perseverance are finally beginning to pay off.

Furthermore, NAME told TAXPAYER earlier this year that the American Kennel Club ran a record number of dog herding competitions in 2020, which indicates that the sport is growing in popularity. This, in turn, will position TWO ENTITIES for growth in the near future.

In light of all this, TWO ENTITIES is clearly moving towards profitability—and that in a poor economy where many people are unemployed and many small businesses are failing.

In any event, "[t]he startup phase of a breeding [or farming] operation may last 5 to 10 years." *Dennis*, T.C. Memo 2010-216 at p. 33. TAXPAYER founded TWO ENTITIES in 2008, roughly seven years ago. However, when the audit started, TWO ENTITIES had been in existence only for about six years. Accordingly, at all relevant times, TAXPAYER was in the customary "start-up" phase, as indicated by the annexed letters in support from those familiar with this type of business. Further, the losses in these early years are, in significant part, attributable to substantial fluctuations in the cost of caring for the livestock on the Farm, including the cost of hay and grain feed. The economic crash and skyrocketing oil prices, which occurred beginning in 2016, stymied travel and increased the cost of everything. As mentioned, upgrading the TWO ENTITIES property with the necessary infrastructure has also presented a substantial cost. The persistently bad economy has posed an unanticipated hindrance to the growth of TWO ENTITIES.

For these reasons, TAXPAYER's prior history of losses at TWO ENTITIES should not be held against her, as the losses were largely the result of factors beyond TAXPAYER's control, and since TWO ENTITIES is still within the customary start-up phase. *Cf. Rozzano*, T.C. Memo. 2007-177 (horse-farming operation deemed to be engaged in for profit notwithstanding steadily increasing losses year-over-year; losses due in large part to fluctuating costs of hay, and business was still in typical "start up" phase for such operations).

(8) The financial status of the taxpayer.

Generally speaking, the existence of "[o]ther substantial sources of income or capital may indicate that a taxpayer does not engage in an activity for profit, especially if personal or recreational elements are involved." *Dennis*, T.C. Memo 2010-216 at p. 33. However, the mere fact that a taxpayer has reaped tax benefits from the activity does not mean that the taxpayer lacks a profit motive, but this fact will be taken into account, along with all the other circumstances of the case. *See id.* at pp. 33-34; 26 C.F.R. § 1.183-2(b)(8).

Conversely, "the fact that the taxpayer does not have substantial income or capital from sources other than the activity may indicate that an activity is engaged in for profit." 26 C.F.R. § 1.183-2(b)(8). Even so, there is no requirement that the taxpayer withdraw from any full-time employment in order to have other pursuits deemed to be engaged in for profit. *See Hendricks v. Commissioner*, 32 F.3d 94, 98-99 (4th Cir. 1994)(internal cites omitted).

TAXPAYER's 2012 tax return indicates that she grossed $181,866 in salary for that year, in connection with her W2 job. Her 2011 return shows $155,976 in gross salary from her W2 job. TAXPAYER also formerly enjoyed high income from various speaking engagements on topics pertaining to animal welfare. Thus, the losses related to TWO ENTITIES have obviously produced sizeable tax benefits for TAXPAYER by enabling her to offset income from these sources.

However, as mentioned above, TAXPAYER is quitting her high-paying W2 job altogether, as of May ___, 2021. Hence, she is now betting everything on the continued growth and profitability of TWO ENTITIES, and the tax benefits of any ongoing losses will be far less than they were when TAXPAYER had significant income against which to offset them.

Even putting aside the fact that TAXPAYER is quitting her six-figure W2 job to devote all her time to TWO ENTITIES, this matter very closely resembles *Rozzano, supra*. The

Rozzano court found that the taxpayer's horse-farming operation was engaged in for profit, even though losses from it offset high income from other sources. The *Rozzano* court noted that the taxpayers, from a financial perspective, could not absorb these losses easily, because the losses consumed between 36 and 48 percent of their income. The court also noted that it was unlikely "that [the taxpayers] would maintain a [mere] hobby costing thousands of dollars and entailing much physical labor," in light of the other factors at play in the case. *See Rozzano*, T.C. Memo. 2007-177 at *8.

As mentioned, TAXPAYER has left her former job at COMPANY and taken up other employment that consumes much less of her time. She has also given up her once-lucrative speaking engagements in order to focus on TWO ENTITIES. Moreover, as discussed, TAXPAYER has sunk more than $350,000 of her personal funds into TWO ENTITIES. Most of TAXPAYER's income from her W2 job has been poured back into TWO ENTITIES, in order to finance necessary improvements without incurring excessive debt. Additionally, the farming and other operations at TWO ENTITIES require TAXPAYER to undertake many long hours of physically grueling labor. Therefore, this factor should not be weighed against TAXPAYER, for the same reasons discussed in *Rozzano*.

(9) Elements of personal pleasure or recreation.

According to the regulations,

> The presence of personal motives in carrying on of an activity may indicate that the activity is not engaged in for profit, especially where there are recreational or personal elements involved. On the other hand, a profit motivation may be indicated where an activity lacks any appeal other than profit. It is not, however, necessary that an activity be engaged in with the exclusive intention of deriving a profit or with the intention of maximizing profits…. An activity will not be treated as not engaged in for profit merely because the taxpayer has purposes or motivations other than solely to make a profit….

26 C.F.R. § 1.183-2(b)(9). The mere fact that the taxpayer enjoys the activity, or derives satisfaction from it, is not alone enough to indicate lack of a profit motive where the other circumstances, on balance, indicate a profit motive. *Storey*, T.C. Memo 2012-115 at pp. 32-33.

As discussed above, any recreational or personal aspects of running TWO ENTITIES are more than offset by the vast expenditures of time, money, and effort that TAXPAYER has incurred and continues to incur in order to grow the business. Thus, this factor should weigh in her favor.

(10). Other matters.

We take umbrage with the examiner's conduct in the course of the audit here. During a phone call between TAX ACCOUNTANT (the EA who prepares TAXPAYER's tax returns) and examiner MR. IDIOT, Mr. IDIOT raised numerous "concerns" which involved nothing more than his second-guessing TAXPAYER's business decisions. For example, Mr. IDIOT appeared to think that TAXPAYER should have simply quit her W2 job (which she is about to do) and gone into debt in order to make the necessary improvements to the property, rather than continuing to work and funding everything herself. He also took issue with the room rates TAXPAYER charges for the Inn, the manner in which she runs the Inn, and the fact that she has not hired more "skilled workers" to assist her with dog-training activities. Put simply, it was not Mr. IDIOT's place to second-guess the manner in which TAXPAYER runs her business. *Cf. Rozzano, supra* (noting that "It is beyond [the Tax] Court's purview to second-guess petitioners' business judgment or the manner of operations of their business."). Mr. IDIOT was also very disrespectful towards TAXPAYER, referring to her as a "rich lady who fiddles with dogs," or something to that effect.

In addition, Mr. IDIOT never bothered to go to CITY and see TWO ENTITIES in operation. 26 CFR § 301.7605–1(d)(3)(iii) states that "[r]egardless of where an examination takes place, the Service may visit the taxpayer's place of business or residence to establish facts that can only be established by direct visit, such as inventory or asset verification." It seems manifest that the manner in which TAXPAYER runs TWO ENTITIES cannot be established or verified apart from a site visit, so we are at a loss to comprehend why no site visit occurred here.

III. Conclusion

For the foregoing reasons, we submit that TWO ENTITIES is a business, not a hobby, thus entitling TAXPAYER to all of her claimed losses and deductions for tax years 2018 and 2019. Please call or email me with any questions.

Statement by Legal Representative of Taxpayer

The undersigned attorney for the taxpayer, with the assistance of other firm counsel and staff, prepared this letter and assembled the accompanying documents. The taxpayer reviewed them for accuracy and truthfulness. The undersigned attorney does not have personal knowledge of the facts set forth herein.

Sincerely,

Tax Pro's Name

Appeal Letter 1

<u>VIA FEDEX</u>

July 15, 2019

Internal Revenue Service
Attn: IRS EXAMINER NAME
Street Address
City, State Zip

Re: TAXPAYER'S BUSINESS NAME AND TAXPAYER'S INDIVIDUAL NAME

Dear Ms. AUDITOR:

This office has been retained by the taxpayers to appeal the examination's findings. This Letter is our formal request for Appeal. Please forward this and the attached documents to the Independent Office of Appeals.

We have reviewed the examiner's conclusions, and the issues we have with the audit include the following:

1. 419 Plan. We disagree with the examiners findings that the plan does not qualify as a valid deduction pursuant to IRC § 419. Even if the plan were disallowed, the taxpayer paid the funds based upon a misrepresentation by CGA, through its agent Thomas Thorndike, and would therefore be entitled to a loss For those funds paid over less anything it managed to recover from CGA.
2. Stock Sales. The taxpayer disagrees with the unreported stock sales.
3. Accuracy Related Penalty. Whether the 419 Plan is upheld or not, it is a highly technical issues and the taxpayer relied on its tax preparer and the letter of approval by the Treasury Department that the CGA plan presented in agreeing to fund the plan. It is therefore inappropriate to apply an accuracy related penalty to the extent the deficiency is due to the 419 plan. Taxpayer's are allowed to rely on technical tax advice from their preparer (United States v. Boyle, 469 U.S. 241 (1985)), and the appropriateness of the 419 plan would certainly qualify as "technical tax advice" that a lay person would not

know, and as such there should be no penalty associated with any disallowance of the 419 plan funding deduction.

We believe the adjustments above are inaccurate. Please forward this case on to the Independent Office of Appeals in Boston, Massachusetts so that we may schedule a time to meet with an Appeals Officer face-to-face and resolve this matter.

Very truly yours,

TAX PRO NAME

C: TAXPAYER'S NAME

Appeal Letter 2

December 21, 2019

Internal Revenue Service
Attn: IRS AUDITOR
Street Address
City, State Zip

Re: TAXPAYER'S NAME SSN: XXX-XX-XXXX

Dear Mr. EXAMINER:

This office has been retained by the taxpayer to represent her in her appeal of the examiner's findings. This letter represents our formal request for an Appeal, so please forward this on to the Independent Office of Appeals in Boston, Massachusetts.

We have reviewed the examiner's conclusions and find the entire exam to be based upon "facts" that are actually wild speculation. The issues we have with the audit include the following:

1. Books and records. The books and records of the taxpayer match the tax return. The examiner appears to have reviewed the taxpayer's books and records and, finding no significant issue, chosen to use the ex-husband's conjecture and an appraiser's wild assumptions as fact, significantly overstating the taxpayer's revenue.

2. The "Business Appraisal." The business appraisal states that it is not even a business appraisal. The appraiser admits that she did not review the taxpayer's books and records, nor did she inspect the premises. Instead she took as fact the ex-husband's statements and using an industry standard set by PetSmart, calculated income that the taxpayer could never have earned. The taxpayer's EA NAME has already detailed these issues in a letter to you, which I have attached and therefore do not see the need to reiterate. Suffice it to say that the appraiser used a soon-to-be ex-husband who had a direct interest in having a high value placed on his former wife's business, and a

big-box retail store that mostly sells animal supplies, as the main source of her information. We therefore find it surprising that the IRS Examiners place any stock in the appraiser's report.

3. Appraiser's "Industry Standard." The appraiser chose to use large retail pet supply stores as her industry standard when attempting to create a basis for why the taxpayer was underreporting. The problem with this is that these stores are not remotely comparable to the taxpayer's business. The bog-box retailers sell few animals but make their money selling animal supplies and food. The taxpayer sells neither supplies nor food, but simply puppies, which have dropped off dramatically since the economic downturn in 2008. As evidence of this is the lack of purchasing she did in 2009 and the fact that one of her largest suppliers also ceased operating in 2009. Again, the appraiser's report lacks any substance that would make us consider it remotely reliable when looking at the taxpayer's business. It relied on conjecture by a highly biased ex-husband and use of unrelated third party businesses to create a picture of fraud that simply does not exist.

4. Civil Fraud Penalty. The use of the civil fraud penalty in this taxpayer's case is improper. Internal Revenue Manual section 25.1.6.1.3 states that:

> "Civil fraud penalties will be asserted when there is clear and convincing evidence to prove that some part of the underpayment of tax was due to fraud. Such evidence must show the taxpayer's intent to evade the assessment of tax which the taxpayer believed to be owing. Intent is distinguished from inadvertence, reliance on incorrect technical advice, honest difference of opinion, negligence or carelessness."

There is no "clear and convincing" evidence to suggest any intentional underreporting by the taxpayer. The only "evidence" at all is an appraiser's report that states the appraiser neither reviewed the books and records nor contacted any third party, and a biased, angry ex-husband's assertions, neither of which is sufficient to assess a fraud penalty against the taxpayer. This is particularly true when we consider that the examiner has been unable to find any reliable third party evidence that shows the taxpayer's numbers to be suspect.

Please forward this case on to Appeals in Boston, Massachusetts so that we may schedule a time to meet with an Appeals Officer and resolve this matter.

Very truly yours,

TAX PRO NAME

C: TAXPAYER'S NAME

Marketing

Marketing Letter – IRS Audits

What to Expect from an IRS Audit of Your Tax Return

Taxpayers can expect a certain level of scrutiny when filing their tax returns, however, some taxpayers may find themselves facing an audit from the Internal Revenue Service (IRS). An audit is a thorough review of a taxpayer's financial records in order to ensure accuracy and compliance with tax laws. It is important for taxpayers to be aware of what an audit entails and how best to prepare for one in case they ever find themselves facing one.

The best advice is to have a tax professional experienced in handling audits represent you so that you do not need to deal with the examiner directly and can get professional advice on responding properly and obtaining missing information.

The first step in the IRS audit process is notification from the IRS that your taxes are being audited. This notification will include information about why the audit is taking place and how you should proceed. You will then need to provide documentation and evidence that supports your tax return, such as receipts, bank statements, Form W-2s or any other forms related to income or deductions claimed on the return.

Once the information has been received by the IRS they will start their review process which typically takes 4-6 weeks but could take longer depending on the complexity of your return. During this time they may also request additional items or contact you directly with questions regarding your financial records.

At the end of the audit process, you will either be notified that no changes have been made or that there have been adjustments that must be made to your return based on their findings. If changes or additional taxes are due, then those must be paid immediately or arrangements made for payment over time.

It is always best to ensure accuracy when preparing your taxes so as not to incur any penalties from making mistakes or misrepresenting information on returns filed with the IRS.

However, if you do find yourself facing an IRS audit it is important to remain calm and organized while providing all requested documentation so that you can successfully complete the audit process without incurring further penalties or interest payments due to delinquent taxes owed. It is also best to not deal with the agency itself directly but to hire a competent tax professional to handle the exam and help you through the process.

Feel free to contact us at (xxx) xxx-xxxx if you have a tax issue with the IRS and want professional help.

Marketing Letter – IRS Offers-in-Compromise

Resolving Tax Debts with an Offer-in-Compromise

Dear _____,

Do you owe back-taxes to the Internal Revenue Service (IRS)? The IRS has several programs to resolve your debt, one of which is an Offer-in-Compromise (OIC).

An OIC is a settlement offer made by a taxpayer to pay less than the full amount owed to the IRS. In order to be eligible for an OIC, the taxpayer must show that they are unable to pay their full tax liability. The financial information provided and reviewed by the IRS will be used to determine how much of a discounted amount they will accept in full payment of the outstanding tax debt.

At [**your business name**], we specialize in offering IRS Representation services, including handling Offers-in-Compromise cases. Our team of experienced professionals are knowledgeable about all aspects of Tax Law and have access to nationwide resources that can help make your experience with us seamless and stress free. We can provide guidance on filing returns, appealing cases and negotiating payment terms with the IRS.

We understand how overwhelming it can be dealing with tax issues, so let us take care of that for you. Contact us today at [**contact number**] or visit our website at [**website URL**] to find out more about our services and how we can help you resolve your debts faster and easier than ever before.

Sincerely,

[Your Name]

Marketing Letter – Penalty Abatement

Penalty Abatement

Maybe you filed a tax return late, maybe you ran into tough times and could not pay the balance in full. Either way, the IRS has applied penalties to your outstanding balance, and you might have noticed that they are not insignificant.

Penalties exist to encourage voluntary compliance by supporting the standards of behavior required by the Internal Revenue Code. For most taxpayers, voluntary compliance consists of preparing an accurate return, filing it timely, and paying any tax due. Efforts made to fulfill these obligations constitute compliant behavior. Most penalties apply to behavior that fails to meet any or all of these obligations.

Penalties encourage voluntary compliance by:

- Defining standards of compliant behavior,
- Defining consequences for noncompliance, and
- Providing monetary sanctions against taxpayers who do not meet the standard.

The IRS will consider reducing or abating penalties when the taxpayer can show either they have reasonable cause for whatever caused the penalty, or they qualify for an administrative relief program the IRS has called "first-time penalty abatement."

First Time Penalty Abatement is an administrative relief program created by the IRS and is provided to taxpayers who are in tax compliance, have made arrangements to pay any outstanding balance, and have not been penalized for the three prior tax years. It is meant as a relief for taxpayers that generally comply and just had an issue come up that caused them to fall out of compliance.

Reasonable cause relief is where the taxpayer can demonstrate that despite his or her reasonable attempts, they were just unable to comply. The burden here is on the taxpayer to provide supporting documentation and paperwork to make sure the IRS can see why they failed to comply and abate the penalties.

If you either have balances that you owe to the IRS and would like to reduce the penalties the IRS has applied, or perhaps you have resolved those balances and would like to have the penalties abated and recover the money from the IRS. Please contact us at (xxx) xxx-xxxx or by email at _____ and let us look at your situation and see if we can obtain relief from the tax penalties.

Marketing Letter – Resolving Back Tax Debts

Options for Resolving Tax Debts with the IRS

Dear _____,

Do you owe back-taxes to the Internal Revenue Service (IRS)? The IRS has several programs to resolve your debt, including payment plans (Installment Agreements) and an Offer-in-Compromise (OIC) to settle the debt for less than he full-amount owed. The IRS may also determine you are unable to make payments and place your account in Currently Not Collectible status (CNC).

The decision on which of these alternatives is best is really dependent upon your financial situation and how much times remains on the ten-year IRS Collection statute. For example, to be eligible for an OIC, you must show that they are unable to pay your full tax liability within the time remaining on the ten-year statute. The financial information provided and reviewed by the IRS will be used to determine how much of a discounted amount they will accept in full payment of the outstanding tax debt.

At [**your business name**], we specialize in offering IRS Representation services, including handling Installment Agreements, having clients placed in CNC, and Offers-in-Compromise. Our team of experienced professionals are knowledgeable about all aspects of Tax Law and have access to nationwide resources that can help make your experience with us seamless and stress free. We can provide guidance on filing returns, appealing cases and negotiating payment terms with the IRS.

We understand how overwhelming it can be dealing with tax issues, so let us take care of that for you. Contact us today at [**contact number**] or visit our website at [**website URL**] to find out more about our services and how we can help you resolve your debts faster and easier than ever before.

Sincerely,

[Your Name]

Marketing Letter – Tax Levies

IRS Tax Levies

Tax levies are one of the most powerful collection tools available to the Internal Revenue Service (IRS). When a person or business fails to pay their taxes, the IRS may impose a levy on their property and assets, such as wages, bank accounts and real estate.

A tax levy is different from a lien, which is also sometimes used by the IRS to collect delinquent taxes. A lien is a legal claim made against a taxpayer's property and assets but does not necessarily result in seizure of those items. A levy, on the other hand, allows for both seizure and sale of those items in order to pay off any unpaid taxes. The amount of money that can be collected through a levy will depend on how much money or property that person or business has available.

When a levy is issued against an individual or organization, they will usually receive notification of this action via mail before it takes effect. This gives them time to make arrangements with the IRS regarding payment of debts owed but it is important to note that if no agreement can be reached within thirty-days then the IRS can proceed with enforced collection measures including seizing wages or bank accounts or filing liens against real estate owned by the taxpayer.

If you have received notice from the IRS about an impending tax levy it is important that you take action quickly as waiting too long could lead to serious repercussions such as wage garnishment or asset seizure. To find out what your options are for resolving unpaid taxes, we recommend speaking with an experienced tax professional who can provide advice based on your specific situation.

Feel free to contact us at (xxx) xxx-xxxx for help on resolving your tax issue and avoiding the impact of enforced collection action by the IRS.

Marketing Letter – Tax Liens

What to Do About an IRS Tax Lien?

What do you do if you owe taxes and there is a federal tax lien filed against you?

Technically the IRS does not need to file anything for there to be a tax lien if you owe money. The statutory lien arises automatically by statute when money is owed the billing notice is not paid. However, because third party lenders and creditors would not know the tax lien exists, the IRS will often file a Notice of Federal Tax Lien ("NFTL") to put third parties on alert that the taxpayer owes the IRS money, and that the IRS has an interest in their assets.

When the government places a lien on an individual's assets, it becomes public record which can have a significant impact on their credit score and their ability to receive loans or purchase items like homes or cars. Some states also require a release of liens before certain transactions can take place, such as the sale of real estate.

A tax lien will remain in place until the debt is paid in full, the tax debt is compromised, or the ten-year collection statute expires.

So, what are your options?

You have several options on dealing with the IRS Tax Lien, not the least of which is to pay the debt in full if you are able. Assuming you are not able to pay the tax debt in full, the options include:

1. Withdrawal of the NFTL. The IRS will agree to withdraw the NFTL if the taxpayer is in a direct-debit installment agreement, has made at least three monthly payments, and the balance owed is under $25,000.
2. Discharging an asset out from under the tax lien. The NFTL is meant to protect the government's interest in the assets. If you can sell an asset and the IRS will obtain the equity (limited to what it is owed) then it will agree to allow the property to be sold.

3. <u>Subordinating its lien to a third party</u>. The IRS will agree to subordinate its tax lien to a third party if the IRS will either obtain cash from the third-party loan, or if your ability to pay the IRS increases because of the new loan (like a refinance of a mortgage).

You have options if you currently have a federal tax lien against you. Contact our office at (xxx) xxx-xxxx and let us see how we can help you resolve your tax issue today.

Sample Blog Entry – Innocent Spouse Treatment by the IRS

Innocent Spouse Treatment by the IRS in Greenwich, CT

The focus of our practice is civil and criminal taxpayer representation, and see many taxpayers who find out about a tax debt that truly belongs to their spouse (or former spouse) in **Greenwich, Connecticut**. There are a few basics you need to understand about **IRS federal tax liabilities** and **innocent spouse** claims.

Most taxpayers realize that there are tax savings when filing a joint tax return with their spouse. However, in signing a **joint return** with their spouse they are accepting responsibility for any liability that flows from that return, both on the return and any additional assessment made later, such as from an **IRS audit**.

Frequently, family law attorneys contact us after the soon-to-be ex-spouses prepared and filed their **joint tax returns** to realize that they cannot pay the **tax liability**. That, or that the spouses have a separation/divorce agreement that states the husband is responsible for any unpaid taxes, yet the **IRS** is pursuing the wife.

A few basics you should understand:

- The **IRS** is not bound by a written agreement the couple entered into, as statute creates joint and several liability for both spouses. The spouse who was not supposed to be responsible pursuant to the court agreement can sue the former spouse, but it will not prevent the **IRS** from pursuing them.
- The outcome will be determined by how much the former spouse knew about the **tax liability**.

The spouse (or former spouse) who wishes to seek **innocent spouse relief** from the **IRS** will need to show that the issue with the return was the responsibility of their spouse and they did not know or had reason to know about the understatement of liability. We represent many taxpayers **seeking Innocent Spouse** treatment, including Appeals and United States Tax Court.

If you have any questions about IRS Innocent Spouse cases or other IRS tax issues in **Greenwich, Connecticut** or elsewhere please feel free to contact me at (203) 285-8545 or by email at egreen@gs-lawfirm.com.

Eric L. Green

Green, & Sklarz, LLC

243 Tresser Boulevard, 17th Floor

Stamford, CT 06901

Ph. (203) 285-8545 x 102

Fax (203) 286-1311

egreen@gs-lawfirm.com

Sample Blog Entry – Mechanics of a Tax Levy

Tax Levy in West Hartford, Connecticut: The Mechanics of an IRS Tax Levy

We focus on tax related issues, including civil and **criminal tax** controversies in **West Hartford** and across **Connecticut** and **New York**. We deal with taxpayers who have fallen into the **IRS Collection Division**'s inventory and are dealing with **federal tax levies** by the **Internal Revenue Service ("IRS")**. A question that comes up often is what can the IRS seize?

There are two types of **federal tax levies** issued by the **IRS**: a **"regular" levy** and a **"continuing" levy**. A **continuing levy** is a **levy** issued by the **IRS** on wages or routinely paid commissions, so it will remain in place until it is released.

A **"regular" levy** issued by the **IRS** reaches the assets owned by the taxpayer at the moment the levy is received. For example: Assume Taxpayer owes the **IRS** $10,000. Taxpayer has $100 in his bank account on Monday. Monday at 3:00 pm the bank receives a **Notice of Levy** from the **IRS** for the $10,000 that the federal government is owed. The taxpayer then deposits $10,000 in his account on Tuesday at 10:00 am. How much does the bank have to send to the **IRS** on account of the **federal tax levy**?

The bank will send the **IRS** the $100, which is the money it had at the moment the levy was received. The $10,000 deposited on Tuesday would not be reached by the **federal tax levy**. The situation is the same with contractors or receivables. The party that receives the **tax levy** only pays over to the **IRS** that amount which it owes the Taxpayer at that moment.

To illustrate this: If a general contractor receives a notice of **tax levy** from the **IRS** for one of its subcontractors, it can only pay that money which was owed to the subcontractor. If the general contractor did not owe the subcontractor anything (because the job was not complete and nothing was owed under the contract) than the **tax levy** would not get anything.

If you or your clients have any issues with **tax levies issued by the IRS** or other **federal tax problems** please feel free to contact me directly at (203) 285-8545 or by email at egreen@gs-lawfirm.com.

Eric L. Green, Esq.

Green & Sklarz LLC

543 Prospect Avenue

Hartford, CT 06105

Ph. (203) 285-8545

Fax (203) 286-1311

egreen@gs-lawfirm.com

www.gs-lawfirm.com

Sample Newsletter

What to do if you cannot pay the taxes?

We know the story: things are tight financially, so you either (1) do not file the tax return, or (2) file the return but don't pay the balance due. But do not worry, you tell yourself, next year will be better. Now it is 2-3 years later, and a letter arrives from the IRS, and the threats start, and maybe it has even gotten to the point of actual levy and seizure activity. Now the IRS is wreaking havoc on your financial life, and you simply do not know what to do.

We know. We have helped many clients through that exact scenario. Fear not, there is a light at the end of the tunnel.

As it turns out the IRS is usually only too happy to work with taxpayers, but there are some ground rules you need to be aware of and a roadmap to follow.

1. Tax Compliance

The first step in resolving your tax issue is to get into "tax Compliance." Compliance means that you have filed all tax returns due for the last 6 years and have made your current tax payments. Once you are in tax compliance, we can now work on resolving the back-tax issue.

2. Collection Alternatives

There are three main collection alternatives to resolve a back-tax debt: Installment Agreement, Uncollectable Status and Offer-in-Compromise.

Installment Agreement

An installment agreement is an agreement to pay the taxes back over time. There are three variations of the installment agreement: Regular, Streamlined, and Partial-Pay. Which type of agreement works best for you will depend upon your personal circumstances and is something we can help you address when you are ready.

Uncollectable Status

Uncollectable status is when the IRS determines that you are unable to make current tax payments. When a taxpayer is deemed uncollectable the IRS may still file a Notice of Federal Tax Lien to secure its position in the taxpayer's assets but will not otherwise take enforcement action to seize (or levy) the taxpayer's assets or income streams.

Offer-in-Compromise

An Offer-in-Compromise is an agreement where the IRS agrees to accept less than the total amount owed to it and the taxpayer agrees to pay the amount negotiated, as well as maintain his or her tax compliance for 5 years following the acceptance of the Offer-in-Compromise ("Offer").

The basis for an Offer is a formula referred to as "Reasonable Collection Potential" or "RCP." RCP is effectively the net equity in assets plus the taxpayer's excess future income for 12 or 24 months, depending upon how the Offer is structured. There can be significant planning done to help a taxpayer maximize the potential for the Offer's acceptance.

If you or someone you know has an issue with paying their federal taxes and needs help to end their IRS nightmare, please contact us by either phone at _____ or email at _____.

Your Name, Firm Info and Address, Phone, and Email

Offers-in-Compromise: Doubt-as-to-Collectibility (DATC)

IRS Collection Document Checklist - Individual

{Please provide us all that apply}

General:

- Have you filed all your federal tax returns? Yes ☐ No ☐
    - If No, which years remain unfiled?
    - Are the tax returns prepared?
- Have you filed all of your state tax returns? Yes ☐ No ☐
    - If No, which states do you need to file in?
    - What tax years remain to be filed?
    - Are the tax returns prepared?
- Has either the IRS or state taxing authority contacted you? Yes ☐ No ☐
    - If Yes, please provide copies of any correspondence you have received

Assets:

- Do you have a bank account? Yes ☐ No ☐ • If Yes, please provide copies of the bank statements for the last six months of bank statements for all accounts
- Do you own any investments (stocks, bonds, mutual funds, etc.) Yes ☐ No ☐ • Most recent statement for all investment accounts (Stocks, Mutual Funds, Trading Accounts)
- Do you have any retirement accounts (IRA, 401(k), 403(b), etc.)? Yes ☐ No ☐ • Copies of all 401(k) and 403(b) plan documents
    - Statements of value for all other investments, including documentation of loans against any investment
- Do you own any virtual currency, or have you owned any virtual currency in the last 6 years? Yes ☐ No ☐
    - Statement of value of anything you currently own
    - If you previously owned virtual currency and sold it please confirm it was reported on your tax returns that were filed with the IRS. Yes ☐ No ☐
- Do you own or have you owned any foreign assets, trusts, or bank accounts in the last 6 years? Yes ☐ No ☐
    - List any foreign assets currently owned

- o If it includes foreign bank or investment accounts, please provide the last 6 months of statements on all foreign accounts
- o If you sold or transferred the assets, please confirm you reported the assets/transactions on your tax returns? Yes ☐ No ☐
- Life Insurance • Statement showing the premium and cash value of life insurance
- Do you own any real estate? Yes ☐ No ☐ If No go to #8 • Printouts for the value of any real estate owned (appraisal, Zillow, etc.)
    - o Recent mortgage statements for any property owned
    - o Recent statement for credit lines/home equity loans secured by any real estate
- Do you rent your home? Yes ☐ No ☐
    - o Lease agreement
    - o Utility bills
    - o Proof of rental payments for the last 6 months
- Do you own 1 or more automobiles? Yes ☐ No ☐ • Kelly Blue Book printouts for value of each vehicle
    - o Recent monthly statement of any loan balance and monthly payment
    - o Recent monthly statement showing the lease payment and time remaining on the lease
- Do you own any collectables (artwork, jewelry, collections, etc.)? Yes ☐ No ☐ • Statement of value or appraisal for collectables
    - o Copy of your homeowners or renter's insurance including riders.

Income & Expenses:

- We need your current income for you and your spouse/partner/significant other you reside with/anyone who contributes to the household income (whether they are responsible or not). Please get us any of the following if they apply:
    - o A current profit and loss for each business or rental activity
    - o If you or your spouse are wage earners, your three most recent pay stubs
    - o Proof of any social security income
    - o Proof of annuity or retirement income
    - o Proof of any child support or alimony received
    - o Proof of any other income or cash flow stream into the household
- Last three months of utility bills

- Proof of your mortgage payment and balance. If you rent, we need your current lease agreement
- Proof of monthly car payments, whether loan or lease, with the balance remaining
- Proof of health insurance and premium amount
- Proof of life insurance premiums
- Proof of disability insurance premiums
- Proof of any alimony or child support you or your spouse pay, including the divorce or separation agreement and court order
- Home equity statement
- Proof of any judgments and payment plans to secured creditors
- Proof of any payment plans with state taxing authorities
- Proof of student loan balances and payments
- Proof of current estimated tax payments (unless you are a wage earner, in which case they are reflected on your paystubs)
- Proof of out-of-pocket healthcare expenses, IF they exceed $52/per person per month (or $114/month for anyone 65 or older)
- Proof of child/dependent care expense, such as daycare and after-school programs
- Proof of any other necessary expenses, such as mandatory union dues, restitution payments, etc.

IRS Collection Document Checklist - Business

{Please provide us all that apply for EACH business owned}

General:

- Has the business filed all federal tax returns? Yes ☐ No ☐
    - If No, which years remain unfiled?
    - Are the tax returns prepared?
- Has the business filed all of its state tax returns? Yes ☐ No ☐
    - If No, which states do you need to file in?
    - What tax years remain to be filed?
    - Are the tax returns prepared?
- Has either the IRS or state taxing authority contacted the business? Yes ☐ No ☐
    - If Yes, please provide copies of any correspondence you have received

Business Information:

Entity Information

- Name_____
- Address:_____
___
- Federal ID Number_____
- Entity Type (Circle One): Sole Prop / LLC / Partnership / C Corp / S Corp / Trust / Estate
- Does the business have employees?   Yes / No
- If Yes please provide us with copies of the payroll information (number of employees, payroll tax returns and if the company is enrolled in EFTPS)
- Does the business utilize a payment processor, like Paypal, Google, etc include virtual currency)   Yes / No
    - If Yes, list them _____
- Does the business accept Credit Cards?   Yes / No
    - If Yes, provide us the list of cards accepted by the business
- Provide us with the names, addresses and ownership percentage of all the owners and officers of the business

- Does the business utilize a payroll processor? Yes / No
- Is the business a party to a lawsuit? Yes / No
- Has the business ever filed bankruptcy? Yes / No
- Do any related parties owe money to the business? Yes / No
- Have any assets been transferred from the business within the last 10 years for less than fair market value? Yes / No
- Do you anticipate an increase or decrease in income? Yes / No
    - If "Yes" explain why

Assets:

- Cash: please provide the last 6 months of statements for all bank accounts
- Receivables: provide a list of all the amounts owed to the business, by whom, how much and how old the receivable is
- Lines of Credit: Provide statements for all lines of credit
- Real Property: Provide a list of any real property owned, its Fair-Market Value, and provide statements showing the amounts owed and monthly mortgage balances.
- Vehicles: List all of the vehicles owned by the business, including the year, make, model and mileage on the vehicles. Also provide statements for any loans outstanding on the vehicles
- Furniture and Equipment: Provide a listing of all the business equipment owned by the business and any loans against it. If possible, please provide a depreciation schedule if you have one.
- Business Debts: Please provide statements showing any balances due and monthly payment amounts.

Income & Expenses:

- Please provide all of the following reports:
    - A profit and loss year-to-date
    - The tax returns for the last three years (or as many years as you have)
    - A current cash-flow statement, if you have one

Consult Letter Regarding Offer and Dissipated Asset Issue

February 1, 2023

TAXPAYER NAME
STREET ADDRESS
CITY, STATE AND ZIP

RE: Consultation re Potential Offer-in-Compromise

Dear Mr. TAXPAYER:

Thank you for engaging us to provide you a consultation regarding your tax liability with the Internal Revenue Service. During the consultation, when we inquired as to where the income which was received during calendar years 2021 and 2022 went, you indicated you made a $200k loan to a new BUSINESS for which you are not an owner of. We believe that this loan is problematic for a number of reasons. Given the loan, we believe an offer in compromise would be nearly impossible because even if the IRS were to agree that the loan is an illiquid asset, they would likely deem it a dissipated asset. Thus, the IRS would include the $200k as an asset and add it to the offer amount[8], as the IRS does this in situations where it can be shown the taxpayer has sold, transferred, encumbered or otherwise disposed of assets in an attempt to avoid the payment of the tax liability.

Moreover, if you were to request any type of installment agreement from the government that required financial disclosure, you would have to disclose the $200k note to the gym. The only way to potentially avoid disclosing financial information would be to pay down the tax debt to under $250,000 and request a non-streamlined installment agreement (NSIA) to full pay the balance within the time remaining on the collection statute. A NSIA must be requested before enforcement or assignment of the case to the field. However, given the close proximity to the collection statute (on or around July 2024), it is difficult to confirm whether a NSIA would be feasible.

---

[8] The IRS will not accept a doubt as to collectibility offer in compromise when a taxpayer shows the ability to full pay the tax debt within the time remaining on the statute. We believe, based on the IRS' offer formula, you would likely show the ability to full pay once the dissipated asset and other factors were considered.

The worst-case scenario would be that the IRS deems the loan/transfer of funds to the gym as a scheme to avoid the payment of tax, which is tax evasion, a criminal offense. They could argue you knew you owed the tax, and you transferred the funds to keep them out of reach of the government. The government could also file a transferee lien against the gym. Transferee liens can be filed where it is established that there has been an actual transfer of property but the taxpayer received no consideration for the transfer. Factors that the IRS may consider in this situation is whether you can prove the transaction was truly a loan. For example, are there executed loan documents, is interest being charged, is there a reasonable expectation that the funds will be repaid, was a UCC filed to secure the loan, etc.

Please let us know if you have any questions. Under the terms of our engagement, this concludes our representation of you in this matter.

Very truly yours,

EA NAME

Cover Letter for Offer – Based on Business Valuation

November 29, 2017

<u>VIA CERTIFIED MAIL</u>

Brookhaven IRS Center
COIC Unit
P.O. Box 9007
Holtsville, NY 11742-9007

    Re: **Offer-in-Compromise for TAXPAYER, SSN X1234**

Dear Sir or Madam:

The taxpayer is filing this Offer-in-Compromise to try and resolve his back-tax debt. Mr. TAXPAYER is desperately trying to turn his business around. However, the taxpayer has had a number of setbacks, most importantly his health issues, which directly impact his ability to run his company. His issues include severe multiple sclerosis, congenital bicuspid, dilated aorta, mixed hyperlipidemia, history of diverticulitis, lung nodule, non-alcoholic fatty liver disease, situational anxiety pertaining to multiple medical issues, insomnia, and glucose intolerance.

Given the medical issues, the taxpayer's out of pocket medical costs are exorbitant. Further, due to his diagnosis of ascending aortic aneurysm, he will need open heart surgery within the next five years to replace both his heart valve and ascending aorta. He undergoes MRIs every 6 months to monitor this condition. Open heart surgery is a very expensive surgery—the taxpayer's out of pocket medical bills will only further increase.

The taxpayer has two children with his current wife, DAUGHTER #1 (4 years old) and DAUGHTER #2 (6 months old). The taxpayer pays $504.47/month for a Florida Savings Account and $313.03/month for Florida prepaid tuition, for his daughter Isabella. The aforementioned expenses are not included in the taxpayer's necessary expenses. The taxpayer also pays CHURCH School for childcare for DAUGHTER, while he and his wife work. The monthly payment is $1,413, which has been included as a necessary expense (and supporting backup provided).

In addition, the taxpayer has a son, TAXPAYER, Jr. ("JUNIOR"), with FORMER WIFE. He pays $1,500/month child support to Ms. FORMER WIFE plus pays for educational expenses, including NAME ($348/month) and NAME Academy ($300/month). He also has a daughter, MORE KIDS, with GIRLFRIEND. He pays $2800/month in child support to Ms. GIRLFRIEND in addition to other necessities (e.g. $1,000 for KIDS's summer school). We have included copies of checks to support that the taxpayer is actually paying these expenses monthly. The taxpayer came to agreements with Ms. FORMER WIFE and Ms. GIRLFRIEND outside of the court system in order to avoid the heavy cost of litigation. However, if he were to stop making these payments, it was agreed that the parties would go to court to have a support order put in place. There are current efforts by the children's mothers to formalize (and increase) the support and submit documentation to their respective child support agencies. The taxpayer has three other children who have attained adulthood, and accordingly, they are not referenced above.

The taxpayer's income has fluctuated wildly in the last several years and so we based the Offer on the recently appraised enterprise value of his company.

If you have any questions or need additional supporting documentation, please let us know. My 2848 is included.

Very truly yours,

TAX PRO NAME

Enclosures

Cover Letter for Offer – Lives with Disabled Girlfriend

<u>VIA CERTIFIED MAIL</u>

November 29, 2017

Brookhaven IRS Center
COIC Unit
P.O. Box 9007
Holtsville, NY 11742-9007

    Re: Taxpayer's Name

Dear Sir or Madam:

This office is counsel to the above-referenced taxpayer, TAXPAYER, in connection with his liabilities, penalties, interest, and other additions for tax years 2010, 2011, 2018, and 2020. As set forth on the attached Forms 433A-OIC and 656, the taxpayer respectfully offers to compromise all outstanding liabilities, for the lump-sum payment of $___. The initial 20% payment and filing fee are enclosed. If this offer is accepted, then immediately thereafter, the taxpayer will remit payment of the balance due on the offer within five months.

Mr. TAXPAYER is in a horrible financial situation. The taxpayer is currently living in a bottom floor apartment that he rents from his mother, MOTHER OF TAXPAYER. He cannot afford alternative living arrangements.

Mr. TAXPAYER lives with his long-time girlfriend, GIRLFRIEND. Ms. GIRLFRIEND has been unable to work for the past four years due to health reasons. The taxpayer provides all of her support and claims her as a dependent on his Form 1040. Ms. GIRLFRIEND was a nurse prior to her health issues—her doctors found and removed a tumor from her spinal cord. She applied for disability after the surgery, but unfortunately had waited too long and was denied twice. Recently, her doctor found two new tumors on her spine and a disc that is dangerously protruding close to her spinal cord; she will need to undergo additional surgery and likely chemo. It is a very difficult situation and Mr. TAXPAYER provides her support and assists in her care.

The taxpayer has made several good faith efforts to resolve his tax issues, prior to filing this instant offer in compromise. He has attempted to enter into installment agreements and previously filed an offer—but his efforts were often thwarted by circumstances outside of his control (for example, a mistake of $210 by his accountant on a return that created an adjustment/new liability or a misunderstanding that he could apply a previous year overpayment to the following year's estimated tax payment rather than delinquent taxes, etc.).

Recently, the taxpayer took out a loan in order to allow him to pay off his high-interest creditor, Capital One, and drastically improve his credit score so he could obtain a new car loan (his previous car had over 350k miles). The new loan had more favorable terms and allows him to focus his energy on remaining in current tax compliance. The taxpayer is dedicated to resolving his tax issues. Please also note there is a loan which appears on his credit union account statements—this loan with the credit union was used to help his pay taxes and the payment of $170/month comes out automatically on the 20th of the month from my checking account. Further, the loan is secured by the balance in the credit union account—this must be considered when reviewing the available equity.

A fundamental purpose of the offer-in-compromise program is to afford struggling taxpayers "a fresh start toward compliance with all future filing and payment requirements." See IRM 5.8.1.1.3.3. As set forth above, Mr. TAXPAYER has been struggling to meet his federal tax obligations. If his federal arrearages are settled as contemplated in this offer, then this will enable him to meet his future obligations and prevent these sorts of problems from arising again. This will redound to the benefit of both the taxpayer and the government.

For these reasons, we respectfully request that the enclosed offer in compromise be accepted. Please call with any questions.

Very truly yours,

Enrolled Agent

Cover Letter for Offer – Medical Issues

<u>VIA CERTIFIED MAIL</u>

November 29, 2017

Brookhaven IRS Center
COIC Unit
P.O. Box 9007
Holtsville, NY 11742-9007

    Re: Taxpayer's Name

Dear Sir or Madam:

This office is counsel to the above-referenced taxpayer, TAXPAYER in connection with her liabilities, penalties, interest, and other additions for tax years 2012, 2013, 2014, 2015, 2016, 2017 and 2018. As set forth on the attached Forms 433A-OIC and 656, the taxpayer respectfully offers to compromise all outstanding liabilities, for the lump-sum payment of $1,140. The initial 20% payment and filing fee are enclosed. If this offer is accepted, then immediately thereafter, the taxpayer will remit payment of the balance due on the offer within five months.

I.   Extenuating Circumstances

TAXPAYER had a long history of payment compliance prior to a horrific car accident in 2002, in which the taxpayer suffered lifelong injuries that have impaired her day-to-day life. Moreover, she had a long history of filing compliance until further problems arose in 2012. Due to extensive brain damage as a result of the accident, Ms. TAXPAYER has impaired cognitive ability, which has caused her to lose her job on a nearly annual basis in the highly competitive field she works in. The constant fluctuation in income and change to independent contractor employment status in 2012 had made it nearly impossible for Ms. TAXPAYER to catch up on her tax debt. She has found some stability at her current job, but the significant travel to Boston and New York puts significant strain on her capability.

Ms. TAXPAYER was involved in a serious car accident on October 26, 2002. She was a passenger in a car that sustained major damage to the right side of the car due to a collision with a tree and a light pole. She sustained severe injuries, including internal brain hemorrhage and lacerations to the right arm and leg. Jaws of life were used to extricate Ms. TAXPAYER. We've included photos of the vehicle—it is hard to believe someone could survive such a horrific wreck.

Ever since the accident, Ms. TAXPAYER's life has never been the same. She sustained severe internal brain injuries which majorly impact her day-to-day life. She has continued word finding difficulty and difficulty thinking. The injury has impaired her short-term memory and cognitive processing.

As the medical reports detail, she suffered from Axonal shearing of the connective tissues in the brain and bleeding. She was unconscious for several days and suffered severely for years having to take speech therapy as well as physical therapy for broken joints in her writing hand and a broken ankle. In 2004-2006, she flunked the Florida bar after four attempts.

Not only has the accident taken a major toll on Ms. TAXPAYER's physical and mental wellbeing—but also her emotional state. She has had bouts of depression, an enhanced startle response, and has less energy. She is also more emotional and quicker to lose her tempter (according to friends and family, Ms. TAXPAYER was previously an easy-going person.)

Due to her dramatic change in personality after the accident, her then-husband walked out on her and their three children. She had to prematurely return back to work before fully recuperating, as she was now a single mother. When she returned to work in late November 2002, she was immediately pressured to generate new business. She was criticized by management that she was too emotional. Her boss fired her for "lack of effort" on March 21, 2003. She had been with the firm 19 years. Ever since, she has been unable to hold down a job for a significant period of time.

As Dr. Knight notes in his medical report, "these cognitive and emotional deficits are permanent and have seriously compromised her ability to practice as a lawyer at the level she was able to perform prior to her accident."

In addition to three doctors' reports, we have included a WSJ article on internal brain injuries which describes how patients are known as the "walking wounded" as the injuries are not external but still real and problematic.

As the article discusses, there are numerous issues (including inability to switch mental tracks), and if not for the medicine she takes from the doctor recommended through the National Institute of Health (NIH), she could not stay awake to work through the day and function. While she works very hard and appears normal, she cannot manage new tasks well.

The repeated loss of jobs in 2003, 2006, 2007, 2009, 2011, 2013 and 2017 took a toll on Ms. TAXPAYER's finances and emotional state. The job she had in 2012 changed her status from an employee with taxes withheld to no withholding and required her to fund extensive national and international travel to try to convince clients to switch firms. She then lost her job again in 2013 and had to start another job in 2014 with no withholding and required her to fund travel to bring in clients. She exhausted all of her pension resources due to job losses and gaps to be rehired and that made catching up with the IRS taxes nearly impossible.

The taxpayer was completely overwhelmed in 2012, starting a job where no taxes were withheld and receiving k-1s in multiple states. Even the CPA she brought them to said he was confused and they were complex and difficult. The taxpayer also lost both of her parents the prior year, after caring for her mother through her battle with liver cancer. It is also important to note that the inheritance she received in 2015 went directly to pay the underpaid taxes from a joint return with her ex-husband that he refused to help pay.

Lastly, Ms. TAXPAYER is also suffering from hypertension and now under medical care from an internist for this medical condition related to the medical damages from the accident. The stress of her tax problems have only worsened the condition.

II.   Attempts to Resolve Tax Issues

Ms. TAXPAYER entered into an installment agreement with the IRS in October 2016. She made every payment timely until she lost her job in August 2017. Prior to entering into the agreement, Ms. TAXPAYER made several steps to bring her living expenses within the IRS standards, including moving from an apartment in Stamford to one in Norwalk. Ms. TAXPAYER was heartbroken to lose her job and deal with her tax troubles once again.

Since the accident, she has not been able to keep a job more than a few years or less (but prior to the accident, she had one job for almost 20 years.) She has had nine jobs since the accident with significant periods of unemployment in between. She has heard "your fired" or "we are terminating you" so many times its numbing. This has been devastating to her (and has been the main reason her case has been in the IRS' inventory for so long). She truly wants to keep her job and be able to continue to make her tax payments. Ms. TAXPAYER has no family to help support her when she loses her job—her parents are deceased, and she has no spouse or significant other.

While she was most recently without steady employment, she did some consulting work for her former employer and withdrew from her small retirement account to pay rent. She started her present job with the Wagner Law Group on September 17, 2018.

Ms. TAXPAYER has virtually no assets – she rents an apartment and owns an 11-year-old Hyundai which is in disrepair. She depleted her small savings due to having no consistent source of income for over a year. With the significant medical and transportation costs discussed below and the repeated job loss, she has no way of saving and making any dent in her tax debt.

III.   Significant Out of Pocket Health Care Expenses

Ms. TAXPAYER's medical condition caused axonal shearing of the brain. She had been taking Provigil to help her focus and stay awake as her brain must work very hard to stay on task. However, the medication has caused side effects for her including having very high blood pressure. This medicine is FDA approved for narcolepsy (sleeping disorder) as it helps people stay awake and focus. Her doctors are now trying to find a comparative medicine to help with her focus so she won't lose another job, while also addressing the high blood pressure. Without her medicine, she goes home at the end of the day and collapses from exhaustion. A new medicine is much needed, but it is unclear what the out of pocket costs will be. Her previous medication was $30/day out of pocket.

The taxpayer is also concerned her out of pocket medical costs will significantly increase once she changes insurance providers. She is currently under a COBRA plan with her old firm because she had better coverage. Once she is ineligible to remain on COBRA in August 2019, the medical plan she will be on with her current employer offers poor coverage and her out of pocket costs will increase further.

Included in the medical expenses is a list of fees pertaining to the upcoming surgery the taxpayer must undergo with Massachusetts General Hospital to attempt to correct the alignment of her jaw which was impacted from the powerful intensity of the accident. She has repeatedly sought medical and dental care for these issues.

IV. Significant Public Transportation Expenses

The travel to Boston and New York for her job puts significant strain on her capability. The taxpayer's firm is located in Boston and a significant client is located in New York City, requiring travel to both locations throughout the month. Not only is it mentally and physically exhausting, but it is expensive. The taxpayer must maintain an older car, pay $360/month for a Metro North train ticket, pay $12/day for train station parking ($264/month) and pay $254 each time she visits the Boston office (which is at least 1-2/month). If she is capable of driving, depending on her medical condition, she pays $60/month in tolls. Accordingly, we have included $938/month for public transportation, but even that may not cover her actual costs.

V. Conclusion

A fundamental purpose of the offer-in-compromise program is to afford struggling taxpayers "a fresh start toward compliance with all future filing and payment requirements." See IRM 5.8.1.1.3.3. As set forth above, the taxpayer has been struggling to meet her delinquent federal tax obligations. If the federal arrearages are settled as contemplated in this offer, then this will enable her to meet her future obligations and prevent these sorts of problems from arising again. This will redound to the benefit of both the taxpayer and the government. The taxpayer prays this offer will be accepted.

For these reasons, we respectfully request that the enclosed offer in compromise be accepted. Please call with any questions.

Very truly yours,

TAX PRO NAME

Cover Letter for Offer – Messy Divorce

VIA CERTIFIED MAIL

November 29, 2017

Brookhaven IRS Center
COIC Unit
P.O. Box 9007
Holtsville, NY 11742-9007

    Re: Taxpayer's Name, SSN X2521

Dear Sir or Madam:

Enclosed please find the Taxpayer's Offer-in-Compromise Form 656, along with the 433-A (OIC) and the checks for the application fee and the first month's offer payment.

The taxpayer has been struggling for years and is going through a very contentious divorce. He would like to resolve his tax issues and put all of this behind him. He is currently an employee of a small company and is having his taxes withheld. There are some particular issues we would like to point out to you when you evaluate the Offer:

1. The taxpayer and his wife are still living together as they attempt to deal with the assets from the family. This divorce has gone on for a number of years and shows no end in sight, so we allocated the joint living expenses per the IRM based upon each of their respective incomes. There is a spreadsheet enclosed that tracks how we allocated for your review. But this is why the income and expense on the 433-A OIC will not add when you review them. We wanted the bottom line income and expense to tie to the allocated umbers so that the Offer calculation would be correct.

2. We listed a value for the company stock of a minority shareholder that right now has no market value. The company has and continues to lose money each year. There is no market for the stock, so we used par value.

3. We have attached an appraisal for the home to calculate the equity available and split the equity between the two joint owners.

4. The _____ Boat is in a trust created by the taxpayer and his wife back in 2000 when times were much better. The IRS filed a nominee lien against the trust, which we disagree with. The IRS's position is that the taxpayer transferred the boat 8 years in advance of having a tax debt. Rather than challenge this position we have included 50% of the value. The appraisal for the boat is attached. It is a wooden boat which requires much more upkeep then more modern fiber glass boats.

5. The taxpayer had his home furnishings appraised at the request of the revenue officer. We have included the miscellaneous artwork from the appraisal on the 433. The taxpayer also has an old 1991 boat with a small rubber dingy which is included.

Please let us know what other supporting documentation you require after you review the Offer, and we will provide it. I can be reached at (203) 285-8545, and my Power of Attorney Form 2848 is attached.

Very truly yours,

TAX PRO NAME

Enclosures

Cover Letter for Offer – Divorce Pending

FEDEX

March 7, 2019

IRS Center COIC Unit
Address

Re: Taxpayer, SSN xxx-xx-xxxx

Dear Sir or Madam:

Enclosed please find the Taxpayer's Offer-in-Compromise Form 656, along with the 433-A (OIC) and the checks for the application fee and the first month's offer payment.

The taxpayer has been struggling for years and is going through a very contentious divorce. He would like to resolve his tax issues and put all of this behind him. He is currently an employee of a small company and is having his taxes withheld. There are some particular issues we would like to point out to you when you evaluate the Offer:

1. The taxpayer and his wife are still living together as they attempt to deal with the assets from the family. This divorce has gone on for a number of years and shows no end in sight, so we allocated the joint living expenses per the IRM based upon each of their respective incomes. There is a spreadsheet enclosed that tracks how we allocated for your review. But this is why the income and expense on the 433-A OIC will not add when you review them. We wanted the bottom-line income and expense to tie to the allocated umbers so that the Offer calculation would be correct.
2. We listed a value for the company stock of a minority shareholder that right now has no market value. The company has and continues to lose money each year. There is no market for the stock, so we used par value.
3. We have attached an appraisal for the home to calculate the equity available and split the equity between the two joint owners.

4. The NAME Boat is in a trust created by the taxpayer and his wife back in 2000 when times were much better. The IRS filed a nominee lien against the trust, which we disagree with. The IRS's position is that the taxpayer transferred the boat 8 years in advance of having a tax debt. Rather than challenge this position we have included 50% of the value. The appraisal for the boat is attached. It is a wooden boat which requires much more upkeep then more modern fiber glass boats.

5. The taxpayer had his home furnishings appraised at the request of the revenue officer. We have included the miscellaneous artwork from the appraisal on the 433. The taxpayer also has an old 1991 boat with a small rubber dingy which is included.

Please let us know what other supporting documentation you require after you review the Offer, and we will provide it. I can be reached at (203) 285-8545, and my Power of Attorney Form 2848 is attached.

Very truly yours,

Eric L. Green

Cover Letter for Offer – Refinanced and Paid IRS Down

<u>VIA CERTIFIED MAIL</u>

November 29, 2017

Brookhaven IRS Center
COIC Unit
P.O. Box 9007
Holtsville, NY 11742-9007

    Re: Taxpayer's Name, SSN X2521

Dear Sir or Madam:

Enclosed please find the executed 433A OIC, 656, and 433B OIC along with supporting attachments. The taxpayer has a judgement by his ex-wife which encompasses the business and his other real estate. He has already refinanced his house and paid the equity to the IRS. The taxpayer also has used business equipment which would not be worth very much at auction and will need it to keep producing income.

The taxpayer has paid as much as he is able to and does not see any way to repay the remainder of his debt, therefore we are submitting this offer.

Please call with any questions. I can be reached at (203) 285-8545. A copy of our Form 2848 is enclosed.

Very truly yours,

TAX PRO NAME

Cover Letter for Offer – Retired

<u>VIA CERTIFIED MAIL</u>

November 29, 2017

Brookhaven IRS Center
COIC Unit
P.O. Box 9007
Holtsville, NY 11742-9007

Re: Taxpayer's Name, SSN X2521

Dear Sir or Madam:

Our office represents the above-mentioned taxpayer, Anil Sehgal. Enclosed please find the executed form 433A OIC, and form 656, along with supporting documentation, and the initial 20% payment and filing fee for Mr. Sehgal's Offer-in-Compromise. The taxpayer is retired and is living off his pension and social security. He lives with his wife who owns their house, and he contributes to the monthly mortgage payments along with utilities. We have included a breakdown of the allocated expenses.

We respectfully ask the IRS to accept the taxpayers offer of $4,006.48. The taxpayer plans to borrow funds from family and friends.

Please call with any questions. I can be reached at (203) 285-8545. A copy of our Form 2848 is enclosed.

Very truly yours,

TAX PRO NAME

Enclosures

Cover Letter for Offer – Failed Business

<u>VIA CERTIFIED MAIL</u>

November 29, 2017

Brookhaven IRS Center
COIC Unit
P.O. Box 9007
Holtsville, NY 11742-9007

    Re: Taxpayer's Name, SSN X2521

Dear Sir or Madam:

Enclosed please find the executed 433A OIC, and 656 along with supporting attachments. The taxpayer once had a successful mattress manufacturing business, with a large contract with BIG BOX STORE. He lost his contract with BIG BOX STORE, which caused him to fall behind with his payroll taxes and stop paying his line of credit with Chase Bank. Chase Bank then later pulled the line of credit and sued the taxpayer personally which caused his home to go into foreclosure and him to file bankruptcy. The taxpayer is now working as a W2 employee.

The taxpayer has just filed his 2017 and 2018 returns, both of which showed refunds due him, though we know the IRS will keep those funds and apply them toward the back tax debt. Mr. TAXPAYER has been struggling financially and his necessary expenses far exceed his income and does not see any way to repay his debt.

Please call with any questions. I can be reached at (203) 285-8545. A copy of our Form 2848 is enclosed.

Very truly yours,

TAX PRO NAME

Enclosures

Response Letter to COIC Analysis 1

August 9, 2019

<u>VIA FAX</u>

Internal Revenue Service
Attn: _____, Offer Specialist
550 West Ford St
Suite 300
Boise, ID 83724-0041

Re: Taxpayer's Name, SSN X2521

Dear Sir or Madam:

Pursuant to your letter dated June 26, 2019 concerning the above-referenced taxpayer, we submit the following:

1.   Income for the prior 6 months:

Enclosed please find the taxpayer's paystub dated July 3, 2019. As you will note, his year-to-date income is $96,923.12. Please see #2 concerning the taxpayer's future wages.

2.   Bank statements for all personal and related business accounts where taxpayer has signature authority:

Enclosed please find the taxpayer's personal bank statements with Capital One Bank. The taxpayer had a failed business, TAXPAYER Associates (it was a sole proprietorship), but it stopped doing business a number of years ago and no longer has a bank account. Also enclosed are bank statements for NAME Biotechnology Inc. The taxpayer has signature authority, but because he is a minority owner in the corporation, has no access to the funds in the bank accounts. NAME is a separate legal entity (C Corporation) owned by multiple shareholders. No cash can be accessed by the taxpayer and all items paid are for strictly business expenses. The company is presently very low on cash—it has over $600,000 in accrued expenses and currently less than $10,000 in cash. It is unlikely the company will be able to continue to pay Mr. TAXPAYER at his current biweekly rate, given the cash flow issues.

3. **Current stock valuation for COMPANY:**

The stock has no market value; only common stock has been issued. The company has and continues to lose money each year. Par value is $.001 per share and the taxpayer owns 10,987,000 shares. Accordingly, $10,987 is an appropriate fair market value.

4. **Current statement showing value of all retirement accounts:**

Enclosed please find statements for Fidelity (x_____) and Citi (x_____).

5. **Provide current statement from your life insurance company showing the cash value of your policies:**

The taxpayer does not have any life insurance with cash value.

6. **Current mortgage statement for house:**

Enclosed please find a copy the most recent mortgage statement with Citizens One and proof of payment (this is the taxpayer's second mortgage). The first mortgage is currently in foreclosure and the taxpayer is attempting to modify. We have enclosed a reinstatement quote from the bank's counsel.

7. **Current vehicle registrations/mileage:**

Enclosed please find a copy of the vehicle registration for the 2014 BMW; it currently has 205,000 miles. The 2000 BMW 323i is not currently registered and does not run; it has 357,000 miles.   The 2007 Honda Odyssey is not currently registered and does not run; it has 270,000 miles.

8.   Current insurance policy for _____ sailing boat:

There is no insurance policy on the boat.

I can be reached at (203) 285-8545 if there are any questions.

Very truly yours,

TAX PRO NAME

Enclosures

Response Letter to COIC Analysis 2

August 9, 2019

<u>VIA FAX</u>

Internal Revenue Service
Attn: _____, Offer Specialist
550 West Ford St
Suite 300
Boise, ID 83724-0041

    Re: **Offer for TAXPAYER, SSN X7985**

Dear Sir or Madam:

The issues that you asked about and requested back-up for are explained below. We have attached the back-up that supports this information.

1.   The Commissions/Schedule C. Mr. TAXPAYER explained he was a 1099 before being offered the W-2 job. He no longer has a schedule C or other income, and he does not receive commissions.

2.   Bank Statements. We have attached the most recent three bank statements. I wanted to point two things out to you:

    a.   The deposits for Mr. TAXPAYER are high for the statement September-October. I asked him about this and he explained that because he was still fighting with New Jersey he held checks before depositing them. After New Jersey was sorted out he went to deposit all his checks and the company asked him to not deposit them all at once. They were all deposited after he made an arrangement with New Jersey. To back this up we have copies of the deposited checks so you can see the dates of the checks that were deposited, as well as a year-to-date earnings statement to verify that there was no additional income beyond his normal paycheck.

b. NY Unemployment. You will note the deposits of NYS unemployment. When the pandemic began Ms. TAXPAYER became scared about their income and tried to find a job, unsuccessfully. New York allows people who are seeking a job to register and obtain unemployment. This she did and ultimately was unable to find a position. The unemployment has since ended.

3. Vehicle. Mr. TAXPAYER was borrowing a car from his brother when the Offer was filed because he was unable to get a loan. Since then he has leased a vehicle for $509 per month. This statement is attached.

4. Address on the Appraisal. I contacted the Taxpayer and asked about the mix-up on the address of the appraisal, because as I said, it certainly does look like his house. He explained that the appraisal was correct. The Village of _____, the area of _____, New York that he resides, recently changed the house numbering in areas due to construction and confusion. He contacted the Village that did provide a letter explaining the change. So his new address is technically _____.

5. Health Insurance. The taxpayer and his family have health insurance through a low-cost state program. They pay $9 per child and $39.95 for each of them, or $134 monthly (copies of the statements are attached)

6. The mortgage balance, as I showed you when we were on the phone, is actually $484,290 (see attached).

Please let me know if you have any further questions or concerns after review the attached materials. I can be reached at (203) 285-8545.

Very truly yours,

TAX PRO NAME

Enclosures

Response Letter to COIC Analysis 3

August 9, 2019

VIA FAX

Ms. _____
Internal Revenue Service
Centralized OIC
PO Box 9011 Stop 682
Holtsville, NY 11742

        Re: TAXPAYER, SSN x6711
                 Offer Number: _____

Dear Sir or Madam:

Enclosed please find the documentation you requested in your SB Letter 2844 (AOIC) dated June 9, 2021 (a copy of the letter is also enclosed herewith). Further, the taxpayer wishes to respond to the following issues:

Income

The taxpayer experienced a temporary uptick in business income in 2020 and the first few months of 2021 due to the pandemic. The taxpayer operates in the building supplies industry—the market surged during the pandemic with millions of people home, doing projects and receiving stimulus payments. Now that people are returning to work and the cost of lumber and other supplies have skyrocketed, his business is starting to return to pre-pandemic levels. He has already lost a significant customer and expects others to scale back as well. It would be unfair to consider the income period during the pandemic as indicative of future earnings, as things are returning to normal. The taxpayer experienced a temporary surge in his industry due to a worldwide pandemic. Accordingly, the taxpayer believes using the pre-pandemic income as reported on his 433AOIC of $12,609/month is appropriate.

The offer analysis is expected to look at a taxpayer's income prospectively—it is an analysis of future excess income (emphasis added). Pursuant to IRM 5.8.5.20, there are "situations that may warrant placing a different value on future income than current or past income..." The IRM further states the IRS should "consider all circumstances of the taxpayer when determining the appropriate application of income averaging." The IRM recognizes there are situations when the IRS must consider the taxpayer's unique situation.

ADDRESS Road

In regard to the property located at ADDRESS Road, the taxpayer has no equity in this property—his former spouse holds a $1.5 million note on the property pursuant to their separation agreement. It was part of a property settlement in his divorce. Specifically, Section 8B of his Marital Separation Agreement dated May 5, 2014 states:

Wife shall quit claim all right title and interest in and to the real estate located at

ADDRESS Road, Mansfield CT. Defendant husband shall execute a promissory note and mortgage deed in the face amount of $1,500,000.00 so as to secure the property settlement referenced supra. All other terms of the note and mortgage deed shall be in statutory form. Husband shall assume any and all indebtedness on this real property and shall indemnify and hold wife harmless therefrom.

Primary Residence

The taxpayer disputes the IRS' valuation of his primary residence, ADDRESS Road, Salem. The value listed on the Form 433AOIC was $171,000. The taxpayer submitted proof that _____ Bank had appraised the property at $171,000. Further, the town has appraised the value at $182,400. The taxpayer's home was built in 1965 and requires updating—for example, it still has the original windows, the original tile flooring (which is cracked and in disrepair), etc. The IRS' value is significantly overstated.

Out Of Pocket Health Care

The taxpayer claimed $220/month in out-of-pocket health care expenses. The taxpayer submitted appropriate backup within the offer package. It is unclear why the IRS is not allowing the $220/month the taxpayer claimed.

Vehicle Operating Costs

The taxpayer should be allowed the current IRS standard of $274/month. The costs of operating a vehicle has increased since the offer was filed, as the IRS recognizes because it increased the standard. Therefore, the taxpayer should be allowed to claim the current IRS standard.

Court-Ordered Support Payments

As evidenced in the taxpayer's bank statements, the taxpayer pursuant to his dissolution, pays $1,500/week to his former spouse. By way of example, in the personal bank statements (BANK xXXXX), the April 24, 2021 thru May 21, 2021 bank statement shows checks written on the following dates: April 30, 2021; May 7, 2021; May 14, 2021; and May 21, 2021 in the amount of $1,500 each. The support payments are significant and can be difficult to manage.

Please call with any questions. I can be reached at (203) 285-8545.

Very truly yours,

TAX PRO NAME

Enclosures

Letter with Offer Payment

August 9, 2019

<u>VIA CERTIFIED MAIL</u>

Internal Revenue Service
PO Box 24015
Fresno, CA 93779

    Re: Offer Payment for Offer # 1001607835

Dear Sir or Madam:

Enclosed please find my Offer payment of $1,000 for the above referenced Offer.

If you have any questions or concerns, please let me know.

Very truly yours,

Taxpayer

Enclosures

Appeal of Denied Offer 1

August 9, 2019

<u>VIA CERTIFIED MAIL</u>

Attn: _____, Offer Specialist
550 West Ford St
Suite 300
Boise, ID 83724-0041

    Re: **TAXPAYER, SSN x2521**

           Offer Number: _____

Dear Sir or Madam:

Enclosed please find the taxpayer's Form 13711, Request for Appeal of Offer in Compromise. We disagree with the following items:

1. **Asset/Equity Table**

    I. **Real Estate, _____, MA**

        a. **County FMV**

    The county valuation used by the IRS does not take into consideration the current condition of the home. The home is outdated and poorly maintained. The taxpayer submitted a Comparative Market Analysis that outlined all of the issues with the home, including an unfinished master bath, damaged flooring, exterior painting that was in disrepair and mice and water damage. Per the CMA, the property was valued at $941,433. The taxpayer recently obtained an appraisal by Cullen Real Estate & Appraisal Company, a copy of which is enclosed herewith. The appraiser personally inspected the property, studied pertinent factors and prepared a formal appraisal. The appraisal report concludes the property has a fair market value of $900,000. Therefore, we submit that the value of the house is $900,000 based the report of the certified residential appraiser.

b. Mortgage Loan Balance

The IRS failed to account for the reinstatement amount owed on the first mortgage of $124,049 and the principal balance owed of $284,227 as well as the second mortgage of $28,516. Therefore, the total mortgage balances owed are $436,792.

c. House, Generally

The amount of equity proposed under the taxpayer's offer is more than the IRS would likely receive by any other way. Given the pending foreclosure, mortgage arrearages and the taxpayer's struggles to get the modification agreement approved, the taxpayer would clearly not be able to refinance the property to tap any equity to pay over to the IRS. If the house goes to foreclosure, the IRS will very likely get significantly less equity out of the house than as proposed under the taxpayer's offer in compromise. If the property goes to foreclosure, the mortgage debt will continue to accrue during the foreclosure process (as well as new debt such as attorney's fees, foreclosure committee fees, taxes, etc.) and there is no guarantee the foreclosure sale would generate 80% of the appraised value. Therefore, it is in the IRS' best interest to accept the offer as contemplated.

2. Income/Expense Table

1. Wages

The IRS failed to account for the irregular wage income of the taxpayer. Enclosed please find a letter from the company's accountant, confirming there are no anticipated funds remaining for 2019 to pay the taxpayer. He is presently receiving no paycheck. The taxpayer is the President/CEO of the company. When the company's finances are strained, his salary is the first to be cut. Therefore, the taxpayer believes it is appropriate to use a three-year average of his income. Pursuant to IRM 5.8.5.20, if a taxpayer has an irregular employment history or fluctuating income, then the IRS should average earnings over the three prior years.

Accordingly, the taxpayer submits his future monthly income is $8,590.39, calculated pursuant to IRM .8.5.20 as follows:

Year	W2 Income
2017	$80,793.00
2018	$96,923.00
2019	$131,538.00
Annual Average	$103,084.67
Monthly Income	**$8,590.39**

2. **Vehicle Operating Costs, Aged Vehicle Allowance**

   The IRS failed to include the additional $200 of operating expense. Pursuant to IRM 5.8.5.22.3, "In situations where the taxpayer has a vehicle that is currently over eight years old or has reported mileage of 100,000 miles or more, an additional monthly operating expense of $200 will generally be allowed per vehicle. Enclosed please find a photograph of the taxpayer's vehicle's odometer and a recent car service invoice as verification as to the car's mileage.

3. **Out of Pocket Healthcare**

   The taxpayer has several ongoing health concerns including respiratory troubles/sleep apnea and he has extensive dental issues. He requires special equipment for his respiratory issues. He needs crowns from his dentist on several teeth; enclosed is the treatment plan he will be undergoing which totals $8,400. Additionally, he is scheduled for oral surgery for implants which will total at least $5,000 (he meets with the oral surgeon next week and will receive a written estimate at that time). Enclosed is verification of these medical payments of approx. $256/month, plus the dental work of at least $13,400, if at best, spread out over 12 months would be another $1,117/month of expense for a total of $1,373/month in out of pocket healthcare expense.

4. **Life Insurance**

   Enclosed please find verification of the taxpayer's term life insurance of $833.35/month.

5. **Current Year Taxes**

Based on the IRS's assertion that the taxpayer has wage income of $13,846, which the taxpayer explicitly denies, the IRS only allowed $2,021/month in current year taxes which is absurd. Based on the IRS income, the taxes would be roughly $3,300/month between the IRS and the state. However, the taxpayer believes his current year taxes are approximately $2,021/month based on his 2018 income or based on a 3-year average as defined above, $2,160/month.

3. **Other Factors**
    1. **Taxpayer's Age and Health**
       The taxpayer is almost 59 years old, is overweight and fighting respiratory issues, has 2 dependent children, and has virtually no savings for retirement. His house is pending foreclosure (if the modification is not approved by the bank) and his marriage has fallen apart due to his ongoing financial issues. The stress of his tax issues is weighing heavily on him. The taxpayer foresees no way of ever repaying his total tax liability, and even the proposed settlement will cause significant financial distress. He prays the IRS will consider his offer as contemplated in the original submission.

After your reconsideration of the taxpayer's offer, we respectfully request the case be sent to the Office of Appeals. I can be reached at (203) 285-8545 if there are any questions.

Very truly yours,

TAX PRO NAME

Enclosures

Appeal of Denied Offer 2

August 9, 2019

<u>VIA CERTIFIED MAIL</u>

Attn: _____, Offer Specialist
550 West Ford St
Suite 300
Boise, ID 83724-0041

    Re: **TAXPAYER, SSN x2521**

           Offer Number: _____

Dear Sir or Madam:

Enclosed please find the taxpayer's Form 13711, Request for Appeal of Offer in Compromise. We disagree with the following items:

1. **Distributions and Wage Income included on Income/Expense Table:**

   We disagree for two reasons: First, the income used was not based on actual cash flow. The IRS must review non-cash income because, pursuant to IRM 5.15, the IRS is to perform a cash flow analysis. Under 5.15.1.16, "Cash flow projections are used by a business to forecast future income to meet upcoming expenses. They are based on comparing money owed to expected revenues. Generally speaking, cash flow is the best measure of a company's profits" (emphasis added).

   In the instant case, the taxpayer's business has debt-financed its operations in the hope the company will begin to become profitable. Though there is income being earned, the secured debts that were needed to get the company going are absorbing the majority of this income. The taxpayer is being forced to pay tax for income that will not be distributed to him and given that the IRM clearly indicates that the taxpayer's ability to pay is best looked at from a cash-flow perspective, we believe it is improper to include this income in the future-income calculation. This is the same rationale used by the IRS for not allowing depreciation, which is an expense that is not really being paid by the taxpayer and so therefore does not negatively impact cash-flow. Hence that expense is removed so that the actual income available to use against the tax debt is taken into account. Here, the company cannot cease to make its debt payments or it will be forced to liquidate, and as it is the sole source of income for the taxpayer, the IRS would go unpaid. Accordingly, we believe it is in the best interest of the IRS to accept the taxpayer's offer of the enterprise value of the company, which the taxpayer will also be debt financing to pay off.

Secondly, we disagree with using the income provided by the business as well as the enterprise value of the business. Pursuant to IRM 5.15.1.23, "When determining the reasonable collection potential, an analysis is necessary to determine if certain assets are essential for the production of income. When it is determined that an asset or a portion of an asset is necessary for the production of income, it may be appropriate to adjust the income or expense calculation for that taxpayer to account for the loss of income stream if the asset were either liquidated or used as collateral to secure a loan" (emphasis added).

Therefore, if the enterprise value is considered in the offer, the wage income (from the business) and the distributions would be excluded. Given that the taxpayer's income has fluctuated wildly in the last several years, we believe it is appropriate to base the Offer on the appraised enterprise value of his company.

2. **Housing and Utilities:**

We disagree with the IRS' exclusion of these expenses. The taxpayer pays these expenses personally. The payment may come out of the business account, but when the taxpayer's accountant prepares the tax return, any personal payments are picked up as income.

3. **Out of Pocket Healthcare:**

Extensive documentation has been provided as to his out of pocket expenses and medical issues. Given the medical issues, the taxpayer's out of pocket medical costs are exorbitant. Further, due to his diagnosis of ascending aortic aneurysm, he will need open heart surgery within the next 1-2 years to replace both his heart valve and ascending aorta. He undergoes MRIs every 6 months to monitor this condition. Open heart surgery is a very expensive surgery-the taxpayer's out of pocket medical bills will only further increase.

4. **Court Ordered Payments:**

   We disagree with the IRS' position that because child support payments are made by a verbal agreement, the payment should not be allowed. In this case, child support payments are made monthly to Carolyn Greenwalt in the amount of $2,800 and proof of these payments has been provided. Therefore, the court-ordered payments expense should be $14,300.

5. **Child and Dependent Care:**

   We have provided proof of the payments the taxpayer has made for his children, including summer school expense, tutoring and education expenses, as well as daycare. We disagree with the exclusion of this necessary expense.

6. **Number of Months Used:**

   The IRS calculated 106 months based on the latest Collection Expiration Statute Date. We disagree with this assertion.

The taxpayer reserves the right to proffer additional objections as they become known. We are requesting an appeal of the denial of the offer and would like to have this case sent to the New Haven, Connecticut Appeals Office, with a face-to-face meeting with a settlement officer.

Please call with any questions.

Very truly yours,

TAX PRO NAME

Enclosures

Letter to Town Clerk – With Lien Release and Payment

August 9, 2019

<u>VIA CERTIFIED MAIL</u>
CITY Town Clerk
Address
City, State & Zip

    Re: **TAXPAYER**
             Address

Dear Town Clerk,

The following document is enclosed for filing on the Connecticut land records:

Certificate of Discharge of Property From Federal Tax Lien

A check in the amount of $60.00 is enclosed for your required fee.

Very truly yours,

TAX PRO NAME

Offers-in-Compromise: Doubt-as-to-Liability (DATL)

FOIA Request – Admin File for Income Taxes

February 28, 2020

<u>VIA FAX: 877-891-6035</u>
Internal Revenue Service
GLDS Support Services
Stop 93A
Post Office Box 621506
Atlanta, GA 30362

    Re: Taxpayer:
            Current Address:
            Taxpayer ID No.:

Dear Sir or Madam:

This is a request under the Freedom of Information Act.

1. **Name and Address**

    Requestor:

    Clients:

2. **Description of the Requested Records**

    The undersigned is the representative to _____. We respectfully request copies of the taxpayer's administrative file for tax years _____.

3. **Proof of Identity**

    As proof of identity, I am including a photocopy of my driver's license and a copy of my Power of Attorney and Declaration of Representative (Form 2848).

4. **Commitment to Pay Any Fees Which May Apply**

    The undersigned is willing to pay for fees associated with this request. If the request shall exceed $100, the undersigned requests to be notified.

5. **Compelling Need for Speedy Response**

    The Taxpayer is in the process of appealing the imposition of penalties related to the failure to file certain foreign reporting forms and the files are necessary to do so.

I declare that the above stated information is true and accurate to the best of my knowledge under the penalty of perjury.

Please call me with any questions.

Very truly yours,

TAX PRO NAME

FOIA Request – Trust Fund Liability Assessment

February 28, 2020

VIA FAX: 877-891-6035
Internal Revenue Service
GLDS Support Services
Stop 93A
Post Office Box 621506
Atlanta, GA 30362

    Re: Taxpayer: _____
            Current Address: _____
            SSN: _____

Dear Sir or Madam:

This is a request under the Freedom of Information Act.

1. **Name and Address**

    <u>Requestor:</u>

    Representative's Name

    Reps Street Address

    Rep City, State and Zip

    <u>Client:</u>

    Taxpayer's Name

    Taxpayer's Street Address

    Taxpayer's City, State and Zip

2. **Description of the Requested Records**

    The undersigned represents TAXPAYER NAME (the "Requestor"). We respectfully request copies of the taxpayers' administrative file regarding his civil penalties under IRC § 6672 for the quarters 6/30/2015 through and including 12/31/2016.

3. **Proof of Identity**

As proof of identity, I am including a photocopy of my driver's license and a copy of my Power of Attorney and Declaration of Representative (Form 2848).

4. **Commitment to Pay Any Fees Which May Apply**

    The undersigned is willing to pay for fees associated with this request. If the request shall exceed $100, the undersigned requests to be notified.

5. **Compelling Need for Speedy Response**

    We are in the middle of an Appeal of these civil penalties and require the information to properly present our case.

I declare that the above stated information is true and accurate to the best of my knowledge under the penalty of perjury.

Please call me with any questions.

Very truly yours,

TAX PRO NAME

DATL Cover Letter – Counted 1099 Twice

August 8, 2020

VIA CERTIFIED MAIL
Brookhaven Internal Revenue Service
COIC Unit
P.O. Box 9008
Stop 681-D
Holtsville, NY 11742-9008

    Re: **TAXPAYER NAME, Doubt-as-to-Liability Offer**
            SSN xxx-xx-xxxx

Dear Sir or Madam:

This office represents the above-referenced taxpayer, TAXPAYER ("Mr. TAXPAYER" or "Taxpayer") before the Internal Revenue Service (the "IRS").

The taxpayer is an independent contractor who does drywall and painting, and in 2018 he worked for a larger contract on a project that he was paid $675,000 to complete. The Taxpayer reported all of this income on his Schedule C when he filed his 2018 tax return – please see his 2018 tax return (Exhibit A) and a copy of the 1099 (Exhibit B).

The IRS, based on our analysis of his transcript, seems to have counted the 1099 twice, and assessed the Taxpayer for the amount due on the second $675,000. See the attached wage & Earning Report from the IRS (Exhibit C) and the billing notice sent to the Taxpayer (Exhibit D). We reached out to the General Contractor who sent the attached letter explaining the total paid was the $675,000 (not $1,350,000 – see Exhibit E).

The Taxpayer gave his accountant the billing notice and the accountant managed to ignore it, blowing the Tax Court deadline so the balance due is not final.

We are filing this DATL and Offering $10 to resolve this matter, as we believe it is fairly obvious this was a processing mistake by the IRS and the Taxpayer does not actually owe this money to the IRS.

You have any questions or concerns after you review this please feel free to contact me at (203) XXX-XXXX.

Very truly yours,

TAX PRO NAME

DECLARATION OF TAXPAYER

Under the penalties of perjury, I, TAXPAYER, declare that I have examined the facts presented in this statement and any accompanying information, and, to the best of knowledge and belief, they are true, correct and complete.

_____ _____

Date TAXPAYER

DATL Cover Letter – Challenging a CSED

August 8, 2020

VIA CERTIFIED MAIL
Brookhaven Internal Revenue Service
COIC Unit
P.O. Box 9008
Stop 681-D
Holtsville, NY 11742-9008

    Re: **TAXPAYER NAME, Doubt-as-to-Liability Offer**
           SSN xxx-xx-xxxx

Dear Sir or Madam:

This office represents the above-referenced taxpayer, TAXPAYER ("Mr. TAXPAYER" or "Taxpayer") before the Internal Revenue Service (the "IRS").

Please see enclosed Form 656-L for the above-referenced taxpayer. We have reviewed Mr. Taxpayer's transcripts (Exhibit A) and believe the collection modules are incorrect. It appears that many of the older periods still open for collection have actually expired. In 2013 Taxpayer submitted a request to be deemed uncollectible. Two months later the IRS deemed him uncollectible, which shows up on both the transcripts and was also noted in his administrative file (see the pages from our FOIA request as Exhibit B). Then 17 months later once again there is an entry to deem them uncollectible.

We respectfully request the IRS to review the modules and correct them so that those that have expired can be fixed and amounts paid in over the last two years properly credited to the current years still open for collection.

You have any questions or concerns after you review this please feel free to contact me at (203) XXX-XXXX.

Very truly yours,

TAX PRO NAME

DECLARATION OF TAXPAYER

Under the penalties of perjury, I, TAXPAYER, declare that I have examined the facts presented in this statement and any accompanying information, and, to the best of knowledge and belief, they are true, correct and complete.

_____   _____
Date   TAXPAYER

DATL Cover Letter – Challenging a Trust Fund Liability

August 8, 2020

VIA CERTIFIED MAIL
Brookhaven Internal Revenue Service
COIC Unit
P.O. Box 9008
Stop 681-D
Holtsville, NY 11742-9008

    Re: **TAXPAYER NAME, Doubt-as-to-Liability Offer**
             SSN xxx-xx-xxxx

Dear Sir or Madam:

This office represents the above-referenced taxpayer, TAXPAYER ("Mr. TAXPAYER" or "Taxpayer") before the Internal Revenue Service (the "IRS"). The IRS assessed trust fund recovery penalties under IRC Section 6672 against the Taxpayer for tax periods ending 09/30/2011, 12/31/2011 and 03/31/2012 due to unpaid payroll taxes stemming from COMPANY Construction LLC (EIN XX-XXXXXXX; "COMPANY"). For the following reasons, we request that the IRS deem the Taxpayer not responsible and remove the improper assessment against him.

Factual Background

Mr. TAXPAYER was an officer of COMPANY along with THIEF ("Mr. THIEF"). Mr. TAXPAYER and Mr. THIEF had a long history of partnership in various business ventures prior to forming COMPANY. Unfortunately, their business (and personal) relationship deteriorated by mid-2011 and it was clear that their partnership was no longer viable.

With the breakdown in two partner's relationship and their irreconcilable differences, Mr. TAXPAYER lost any and all financial control he had over COMPANY. Once Mr. TAXPAYER lost trust in Mr. THIEF after he believed Mr. THIEF was improperly allocating funds/stealing from COMPANY[9]; Mr. TAXPAYER confronted Mr. THIEF about his actions and Mr. THIEF quickly became irascible. Mr. TAXPAYER was intimated by Mr. THIEF and feared further retaliation and future altercations. Mr. THIEF refused to disclose anything about the finances from that point forward and became verbally abusive and aggressive when Mr. TAXPAYER inquired.

As a result of Mr. TAXPAYER's fear of Mr. THIEF's erratic behavior (and quite frankly, fear of his anger turning into physical violence), Mr. TAXPAYER stopped going to the office building by the end of second quarter 2011. As Mr. TAXPAYER ceased going to the office out of fear, he had no knowledge of when checks were delivered/payments came in. Therefore, he didn't know when funds would be deposited into the bank account (in order to make any federal tax payments or payments otherwise). Further, as soon as there were funds in the bank account, Mr. THIEF immediately directed them to be spent. Mr. THIEF retained all financial control over COMPANY, as sworn to in Exhibit A, the affidavit of Ms. MANAGER ("MANAGER Affidavit"). Ms. MANAGER was the office manager for COMPANY and had first-hand knowledge over the financial activities of COMPANY. While Mr. TAXPAYER had signatory authority over the bank accounts of the business – he had no control over the accounts because Mr. THIEF left no funds in the account. Mr. TAXPAYER had no knowledge or familiarity with the company's cash flow or books and records because he was completely shut out of the business by Mr. THIEF. Mr. TAXPAYER feared retaliation and intense altercations when he would try to inquire.

Mr. TAXPAYER made a formal request via the Freedom of Information Act in order to review his administrative file and determine how and why he was assessed the trust fund recovery penalty. As of the date of this letter, Mr. TAXPAYER has not received a response. The undersigned and the Taxpayer were provided some verbal information from the current revenue officer assigned to the case, but she was not involved in the original trust fund investigation and had little information concerning same. Mr. TAXPAYER was told that the IRS's records suggest that he signed the Form 4180. If

---

[9] Upon information and belief, Mr. TAXPAYER believes Mr. THIEF diverted funds that belonged to COMPANY to his own company, THIEF Construction, LLC ("CC"). CC and Mr. THIEF were embattled in various litigation and collection lawsuits during 2011-2013 and funds were being diverted from COMPANY to stave off creditor action against CC. Enclosed as Exhibit C is verification of the pending lawsuits during the relevant time period against CC and Mr. THIEF.

Mr. TAXPAYER, close to ten years ago, was presented a pre-filled 4180 by a revenue officer for his signature, there was no intentional acknowledgment that he was waiving any protest to the determination that he was a responsible party. Rather, it was a misunderstanding of the circumstances as presented. During this time period (2012), Mr. TAXPAYER was in poor mental health as a result of the intimidation actions by Mr. THIEF and his failed business.

Enclosed as Exhibit B are email communications between Mr. TAXPAYER and Mr. THIEF that prove that Mr. THIEF had the locks to the office changed and did not provide Mr. TAXPAYER a new key. While the stated reason by Mr. THIEF is that there were burglaries, the MANAGER Affidavit contradicts that reason. Mr. TAXPAYER believes the locks were changes to prevent him from entering the office. The MANAGER Affidavit further corroborates that Mr. TAXPAYER was powerless to make any payments as he saw fit. Accordingly, the determination that Mr. TAXPAYER as a responsible party is erroneous, and should be reconsidered.

Lastly, upon learning of the balance owed to the IRS by COMPANY, Mr. TAXPAYER has made countless attempts over the years to liquidate the one remaining asset of COMPANY in order to pay the IRS. COMPANY had funds escrowed with a law firm that could only be liquidated if both Mr. TAXPAYER and Mr. THIEF signed off on it (pursuant to the escrow agreement). Once Mr. TAXPAYER learned of the IRS liability, he requested the funds be liquidated to pay the IRS. However, Mr. THIEF refused to consent. Therefore, even though the business stopped operating in 2012, funds remained in the law firm's escrow account until 2021, when, upon much effort on behalf of the Taxpayer, he was able to have the IRS levy the law firm's escrow account and receive the funds. Without the cooperation and insistence of the Taxpayer, the IRS would not have received the payment. In fact, the revenue officer was informed by a supervisor that she could not issue levies on behalf of COMPANY (as she was only assigned Mr. TAXPAYER's case); the undersigned's office elevated the issue to ensure the IRS received the funds it was owed.

Law and Argument

Internal Revenue Code § 6672 provides the following:

> Any person required to collect, truthfully account for, and pay over any tax imposed by this title who willfully fails to collect such tax, or truthfully account for and pay over such tax, or willfully attempts in any manner to evade or defeat any such tax or the payment thereof, shall, in addition to other penalties provided by law, be liable to a penalty equal to the total amount of the tax evaded, or not collected, or not accounted for and paid over.

26 U.S.C. § 6672. Thus, trust fund recovery penalties may be imposed on individuals who: (1) were required to collect, account for, and pay over trust fund taxes; and (2) willfully failed to do so. "The person against whom the IRS assesses a § 6672 tax penalty has the burden of disproving, by a preponderance of the evidence, the existence of one of these two elements." Fiatarulo v. United States, 8 F.3d 930, 938 (2d Cir. 1993).

Based on the facts and circumstances in the instant case, Mr. TAXPAYER could not have willfully failed to pay the payroll taxes as he had no authority to make that decision. He was locked out of the office and locked out of the company's finances. Mr. TAXPAYER was unaware that COMPANY still had employees—after the partners' falling out, on or around August 2011, Mr. TAXPAYER asked Mr. THIEF to wind down/shut down the company. It is inequitable to maintain that Mr. TAXPAYER should be held liable for taxes that he could not choose to pay from a company whose financials he had no access to utilize.

In Winter v. U.S., 196 F.3d 339 (1999), the U.S. Court of Appeals for the Second Circuit held that the U.S. District Court for the Southern District of New York erred in granting the IRS's motion for summary judgment with respect to whether an officer, director, and shareholder of a company was a responsible person within the meaning of IRC § 6672, as genuine issues of material fact existed. Rita Romer served as corporate secretary of two entities, and was owner of 20% of the stock of one entity. The IRS assessed penalties under § 6672 against the president, vice president, and controller of the entities, along with Rita. In analyzing the first element – i.e. whether Rita was properly characterized as a responsible party - the court set forth a number of factors to consider, including whether the individual:

(1) is an officer or member of the board of directors, (2) owns shares or possesses an entrepreneurial stake in the company, (3) is active in the management of day-to-day affairs of the company, (4) has the ability to hire and fire employees, (5) makes decisions regarding which, when and in what order outstanding debts or taxes will be paid, (6) exercises control over daily bank accounts and disbursement records, and (7) has check-signing authority.

Id. (citing United States v. Rem, 38 F.3d 634, 642 (2d Cir. 1994). And, in looking to the second element of § 6672, the court noted that "willfulness" means a person who (a) knew of the company's obligation to pay withholding taxes, and (b) knew that company funds were being used for other purposes instead. Rem, 38 F.3d at 643.

Ultimately, the court held that, although Rita was an officer, director, and shareholder of one of the entities, she had presented sufficient evidence to show that her ownership interest and titles were a mere convenience to the entity's president. Further, while the IRS introduced evidence that Rita had check-signing authority, she countered with evidence that she had virtually no power to sign a check without the knowledge or consent of either the entity's president or vice president. Accordingly, the district court erred in holding that Rita was a responsible party as a matter of law.

Here, Mr. TAXPAYER does not fall within either element of § 6672. Applying the above-mentioned factors with respect to who may be deemed a "responsible party," Mr. TAXPAYER was unable to make decisions regarding which, when and in what order outstanding debts or taxes would be paid, as substantiated by the MANAGER Affidavit. Mr. TAXPAYER did not exercise control over daily bank accounts or disbursement records (he was both literally and figuratively locked out of the office). Rather, the payroll tax returns were prepared for and signed by Mr. THIEF. Further, while Mr. TAXPAYER had check-signing authority over the bank account, that authority was limited because there were no funds in the account for Mr. TAXPAYER to effectuate payment on his own (the funds would be transferred or spent as soon as they were deposited). Mr. TAXPAYER made no decisions on hiring and firing of employees (he asked COMPANY to be shut down and that request was ignored).

With respect to the willfulness element, Mr. TAXPAYER did not have knowledge that the company's funds were being used for purposes other than fulfilling the company's obligation to pay withholding taxes. When Mr. TAXPAYER first became aware that the company was experiencing cash flow issues, he approached Mr. THIEF, who immediately became irascible.

Mr. TAXPAYER requested that Mr. THIEF shut down COMPANY to avoid incurring any more debt on the company, but Mr. THIEF refused and threatened him.

As Mr. TAXPAYER was locked out of the office building and Mr. THIEF shared no information with him concerning the unpaid tax liabilities, Mr. TAXPAYER believed there were either no employees or the taxes were being paid. He realized that was an inaccurate belief only when the revenue officer subsequently contacted him. And, to reiterate, Mr. TAXPAYER would have had no ability to remedy any non-payment unilaterally, as he was unable to exercise control over the company's finances due to Mr. THIEF's behavior. Accordingly, Mr. TAXPAYER does not meet the definition of willfulness under IRC § 6672 as he had neither knowledge of the unpaid taxes nor any ability to control the payment of the taxes.

IV. CONCLUSION

Mr. TAXPAYER should not have been deemed liable for the taxes that he could not control nor influence. He had no access to the company's financials, and no ability to make determinations as to which payments would be made. Accordingly, any non-payment of the payroll taxes on his part could not have been willful and we request that Mr. TAXPAYER be deemed not responsible for COMPANY Construction LLC's liability. Mr. TAXPAYER respectfully requests the right to supplement this filing upon receipt of the IRS' administrative file.

Very truly yours,

TAX PRO NAME

C. D. TAXPAYER

DECLARATION OF TAXPAYER

Under the penalties of perjury, I, TAXPAYER, declare that I have examined the facts presented in this statement and any accompanying information, and, to the best of knowledge and belief, they are true, correct and complete.

_____   _____
Date   TAXPAYER

Fax Letter – Withdrawal Because They Will Abate

January 21, 2020

To: Ms. IRS EMPLOYEE
From: Tax Pro

Re: TAXPAYER NAME

Dear Ms. IRS EMPLOYEE:

Enclosed please find the Taxpayer's Form 14773 to withdraw his Doubt-as-to-Liability Offer. We just want to reiterate that the taxpayer is agreeing to this because you have agreed to abate the incorrect 1099 income and correct his tax liability.

If for some reason you are unable to correct the liability as we discussed the Taxpayer intends to proceed with his Offer.

I can be reached at (203) XXX-XXXX if you have any questions.

Very truly yours,

TAX PRO NAME

Onboarding

Onboarding Workflow

1. Client information taken on Intake Form
2. Intake Form Circulated to Confirm We Want the Case
3. Consult Agreement Sent
4. Payment for Consult Received
5. Client Set-Up in Inventory case Tracking
6. Consult Scheduled
7. Does client want to hire us?
    a. Yes – See #5
    b. No, Close File
8. Retainer Agreement and POA sent to Client
9. Move the client into the Service Line Required

Client Intake Form

Personal Information:

    Name: _____

    Telephone Number: _____

    Email: _____

    Who referred you to us? _____

    Who is your tax preparer? _____

I need tax help with:

    _____ Internal Revenue Service (IRS)

    _____ State (which one) _____

Define tax matter:

    Personal Income Tax

    Corporate, Partnership or other entity

    Trusts and Estates

    Foreign

    Cryptocurrency

    Tax planning

Have you received any written communications from the taxing authority?

Yes_____ No _____

Please attach the most recent correspondence from the taxing agency. [Completion of the form or submission of correspondence does not establish an attorney/client relationship.]

Conflict Waiver Form

Via Email

July 1, 2021

Client Names
Client Address
City, State and Zip

Re: Potential Conflict of Interest and Waiver

Dear Mr. CLIENT and Mrs. CLIENT

Your tax returns for the year(s) _____ are currently under examination by the Internal Revenue Service ("IRS"). Having reviewed your records and spoken with you we believe there is a chance that the IRS will make adjustments to your tax returns. These adjustments will create tax liabilities that, because you filed joint tax returns, you will both be responsible for joint and severally.

We spoke with you and explained that the adjustments look like they will be due to _____'s business, and therefore _____ has a potential innocent spouse defense to this liability. This creates a potential conflict of interest for us to continue representing both of you during this audit, and pursuant to our ethics rules, we have recommended to you that _____ seek independent representation in this matter.

In signing this letter, you are acknowledging that we have recommended that _____ seek independent representation, that you have chosen not to seek independent representation, and you are waiving this conflict of interest and want us to continue representing both of you in this matter.

Very truly yours,

TAX PRO NAME

Acknowledged and Consented

_____   _____
Taxpayer Spouse 1   Taxpayer Spouse 2

Retainer Agreement – Hourly

Via Email

July 1, 2021

Client Names
Client Address
City, State and Zip

Re: Client Retention Agreement

Dear Clients name:

We are pleased you have requested that Your firm's name provide you with representation as set forth below. We would appreciate receiving written acknowledgement of this agreement for our files. The Bar recommends that there be a written fee agreement between attorneys and their clients. Additionally, we feel that it is in the best interest of our clients that they be fully informed of our billing practices. The purpose of this letter, therefore, is to set forth the scope of our engagement as legal counsel to you, to set forth the financial arrangements regarding our engagement and to verify our agreement of the foregoing:

1.   Scope of Engagement

Subject to the terms and conditions herein, including without limitation advance payment of the retainer and a signed copy of this agreement your firm's name will perform those legal services which you requested and, more specifically, to represent you and your company before the Internal Revenue Service (the "Engagement").

2.   Fee for Representation

Our billing practice is to charge for our services based on the hourly rate of the attorney involved. We bill in increments of no less than 1/10 of one hour. Please note, we bill for all services our office provides, including but not limited to: correspondence, telephone calls, document preparation, legal research, electronic legal research, inter-office conference, depositions, trials, meetings, etc. We use the amount of time devoted to a matter by a particular attorney at that attorney's hourly rate. These hourly rates are based upon experience, expertise and standing. In addition, we try to use associate, paralegal, legal assistant and/or secretarial support on projects whenever possible. All hourly rates are reviewed from time to time and may be adjusted and/or increased without notice. It is likely that all of these hourly rates will be increased annually usually commencing at the beginning of each calendar year and you hereby consent to such increase. My hourly rate is $500/hour. Our firm's rates for staff range from $75 - $275/hour, and for partners from $350 - $550/hour.

The detail and the monthly statement will inform you not only of the fees and disbursements incurred but also of the nature and progress of the work performed. These statements are due and payable upon receipt, but in any event, no later than thirty days thereafter. We reserve the right to charge interest at an appropriate rate (currently I% per month) calculated monthly starting forty-five days after issuance of the statement and continuing until fully paid. You will be sent monthly billing statements as to work performed. We generally bill clients on either the 1st or 15th of the month. If you have a preference as to when you receive a bill, please let me know.

We do our best to see that our clients are satisfied not only with our services but also with the reasonableness of the fees and disbursements charged for these services. Therefore, if you have any questions about or objection to a statement or the basis for our fees to you, you should raise it promptly and not more than thirty (30) days after you receive a bill for discussion. If you object only to a portion of the statement, we ask you pay the remainder, which will not constitute a waiver of your objections.

3. **Disbursements**

The performance of legal services involves costs and expenses, some of which must be paid to third parties. These expenses include, but are not limited to, filing fees, court reporters, deposition fees, travel costs, copying costs, telecopier costs, messenger services, long distance telephone charges, computerized research expenses and expenses of experts whom we deem appropriate to assist in our representation of you. We do not charge for internal copying costs, but if a production job is large and must be sent out we will charge you the actual expense. We expect that you will either pay directly or reimburse us for such costs. If such costs may be calculated beforehand and appear to be substantial, we may ask you to advance us those sums before we expend them or to reimburse the vendor directly.

4. **Retainer**

We will require a payment of $5,000.00 prior to commencement of work on Your behalf, the amount to be determined at that time depending upon the scope of the work you require. Should the Engagement require work beyond the anticipated scope, we may require an additional retainer be paid. If the retainer is exhausted and you receive a bill, please pay the amount due. At the conclusion of the Firm's representation of You, any remaining positive retainer balance will be returned to You. You also agree that the retainer payment may be deposited in the Firm's general operating account and comingled with other funds.

Please note, we have tried to keep the retainer amount as low as possible, however, given the nature and complexity of the Engagement, it is possible that the retainer amount may be exceeded.

5. **Withdrawal from Representation**

The attorney client relationship is one of mutual trust and confidence. If you, for whatever reason, wish us to cease representing you, you may request that we do so. If we feel we no longer wish to represent you, we will request that the court (if an appearance has been filed) to permit us to terminate our representation of you. We will only do so in the following circumstances: (a) a lack of cooperation by you in promptly submitting necessary requested information; (b) your knowingly providing us, your adversaries or the court with false information; (c) your disregard of advice about matters of critical importance to your case; (d) your failure to promptly pay legal fees; or (e) for any other reason provided advance notice is provided.

Upon such termination, however, you would remain liable for any unpaid fees and costs. We also shall be authorized to reveal this agreement and any other necessary documents to any court or agency if the same should prove necessary to effect withdrawal or collection of our fees.

It is the policy of this firm to make every effort to have our clients feel that they are treated on a fair basis. We welcome an honest discussion of our fees and our services and encourage our clients to inquire about any matter relating to our fee arrangement or monthly statements that are in anyway unclear or appear unsatisfactory. If you have any questions, please do not hesitate to call us.

6.   Conflict Waiver

As I have explained to You, there may, at times, be potential conflicts of interest among the various business and/or individuals jointly represented by the Firm. I have reviewed these facts with You, after due consideration, believe we can properly represent all the parties. By signing this letter you confirm this and agree that you hereby voluntarily and knowingly waive any conflict of interest that may have existed or may exist now. You also are confirming that if an actual conflict arises in the future that you understand we would be required to withdraw from representing you and the other parties in the conflict and that you would all need to seek independent representation.

7.   Future Services

This agreement will also apply to services rendered for such future matters that we agree will be handled by the Firm. If, however, such services, are substantially different from those to which this agreement applies (for instance, an appearance on your behalf in court), either party may request that a new agreement be executed, or that this agreement be reacknowledged.

If this letter correctly sets forth your understanding of the scope of the services to be rendered to the company by the Firm, and if the terms of the engagement are satisfactory, please execute the enclosed copy of this letter and return it us. If the scope of the services described is incorrect or if the terms of the engagement set forth in this letter are not satisfactory to you, please let us know in writing so that we can discuss either aspect.

By executing this agreement, you acknowledge that there is uncertainty concerning the outcome of this matter and that the Firm and the undersigned attorneys have made no guarantees as to the disposition of any phase of this matter. All representations and expression relative to the outcome of this matter, are only expressions of the said attorney's opinions and do not constitute guarantees. We look forward to continuing to work with you and thank you once again for the opportunity to serve.

Very truly yours,

TAX PRO NAME

READ, AGREED AND CONSENTED TO:

COMPANY NAME

_____   _____

Client Name, Position   Date

_____   _____

Client Name, Individually   Date

Retainer Agreement – Flat Fee

Via Email

July 1, 2021

Client Names
Client Address
City, State and Zip

Dear Taxpayer:

This letter is to confirm and specify the terms of our engagement with you and to clarify the nature and extent of the services we will provide. In order to ensure an understanding of our mutual responsibilities, we ask all clients to confirm the following arrangements.

We will prepare a federal Offer-in-Compromise ("OIC") from information that you will furnish us. We will not audit or otherwise verify the data you submit beyond the back-up documents you supply us to submit to the IRS the Collection Information Statements ("CIS") as part of the OIC, although it may be necessary to ask you for clarification of some of the information. We will furnish you with questionnaires and/or worksheets to guide you in gathering the necessary information. Your use of such forms will assist in keeping pertinent information from being overlooked.

It is your responsibility to provide all the information required for the preparation of complete and accurate financial forms for the OIC. You should retain all the original documents, canceled checks and other data that form the basis of the information for the CIS forms. These may be necessary to prove the accuracy and completeness of the forms to the IRS. You have the final responsibility for the information reported on the CIS forms and, therefore, you should review them carefully before you sign them.

Our fee for preparing and filing the OIC for the IRS will be a flat fee of $5,000. This amount is payable prior to our beginning work. If you paid a consultation fee then it is our practice to reduce the flat fee for the consultation fee already paid. You will be responsible for the IRS fee for applying for the OIC and any OIC payment required with the OIC.

Our work in connection with the preparation of your OIC does not include any procedures designed to discover defalcations or other irregularities, should any exist. If requested we will render such accounting and bookkeeping assistance as determined to be necessary for preparation of the OIC, including missing tax returns, which will be a separate engagement and will be billed separately.

During the time your OIC is pending, and if accepted, for the five years following you will be required to maintain your tax compliance, which means that all tax returns are filed timely (including extensions) and that all taxes are paid timely. Timely payment of taxes for self-employed individuals means on a quarterly basis based upon the schedule laid out in the IRS 1040-ES Form and Instructions. For wage earners it means that you are having sufficient withholding taken so there will be no liability at the end of the year. For business clients it means your payroll taxes are deposited on schedule.

We are familiar with the OIC process and will do our best to obtain the result you want, however, the acceptance of an OIC is at the IRS's discretion, and because of that we cannot guarantee results.

Any tax refunds owed to you while the Offer is pending and for the year in which the Offer is accepted will be kept by the IRS. Also, all tax attributes (capital gains carryovers, net operating losses, etc) you have will be reduced to zero as part of the OIC acceptance agreement.

You should be aware that you are submitting the OIC, and signing the CIS forms that support it, under penalty of perjury. The IRS will consider the failure to disclose any assets of the creation of false information or documents a federal crime punishable by fine, incarceration, or both. The IRS Centralized Offer in Compromise Unit will investigate your Offer and the information provided. It is therefore critical that what you provide be accurate. You should also know that as part of the investigation process for your OIC the IRS may review your tax returns and may refer your case to the examination division for an audit.

Our fee for the preparation of the OIC is limited to the OIC submission and review process. You are responsible for any application fees and payments toward the OIC. If the OIC is rejected, you will be provided thirty days to file an Appeal. We often find we need to go to Appeals to get the OIC accepted. Any decision to go to Appeals will be done in conjunction with you and these services will be billed based upon the amount of time required at standard billing rates plus out-of-pocket expenses. We retain the right to request funds be paid in as a retainer up front to cover this work, and all invoices are due and payable upon presentation.

If the foregoing fairly sets forth your understanding, please sign the enclosed copy of this letter in the space indicated and return it to our office. However, if there are other services you expect us to perform, please inform us so we can correct and update this letter.

We want to express our appreciation for this opportunity to work with you.

SINCERELY,

TAX PRO NAME

CLIENT SIGANTURE

Accepted By: _____

Date: _____

Retainer Agreement – Consult

Via Email

July 1, 2021

Client Names
Client Address
City, State and Zip

RE: Fee Agreement for Representation for the Limited Purpose

Dear Taxpayer:

You have requested and Green & Sklarz LLC (the "Firm") has agreed to represent you with regard to the following legal service(s) only:

Consultation on your tax matter (the "Matter")

The scope of the Firm's representation of you will consist of a single consultation at which we will review the Matter and give our advice to you. Upon completion of the consultation, the Firm will no longer be your lawyer. Any future legal services will require a separate retainer agreement.

The Firm's fee for this service shall be $950.00.

By executing this agreement, you acknowledge that there is uncertainty concerning the outcome of this matter and that the Firm and the undersigned attorneys have made no guarantees as to the disposition of any phase of this matter. All representations and expression relative to the outcome of this matter, are only expressions of the said attorney's opinions and do not constitute guarantees.

AGREED AND ACCEPTED

_____   _____
Client Name   Date

_____   _____
Rep's Name   Date

Retainer Agreement – Streamlined IA with FTA

Via Email

July 1, 2021

Client Names
Client Address
City, State and Zip

RE: Fee Agreement for Representation for the Limited Purpose

Dear Taxpayer:

You have requested and _____ LLC (the "Firm") has agreed to represent you with regard to the following legal service(s) only:

To request an installment agreement with the Internal Revenue Service and seek first time penalty abatement on tax year 20____ (the "Matter")

The scope of the Firm's representation of you will consist of the Matter, as described above at which we will review the Matter and explain its terms to you. Upon completion of the Matter, the Firm will no longer be your representative. Any future services will require a separate retainer agreement.

The Firm's fee for this service shall be $1,000.00.

By executing this agreement, you acknowledge that there is uncertainty concerning the outcome of this matter and that the Firm and the undersigned representatives have made no guarantees as to the disposition of any phase of this matter. All representations and expression relative to the outcome of this matter, are only expressions of the said representative's opinions and do not constitute guarantees.

AGREED AND ACCEPTED

_____   _____
Client Name   Date

_____   _____
Rep's Name   Date

Retainer Agreement – Transcript Analysis

Via Email

July 1, 2021

Client Names
Client Address
City, State and Zip

RE: Fee Agreement for Representation for the Limited Purpose

Dear Taxpayer:

You have requested and _____ LLC (the "Firm") has agreed to represent you with regard to the following legal service(s) only:

Pull Internal Revenue Service transcripts for transcript analysis (the "Matter")

The scope of the Firm's representation of you will consist of the Matter, as described above at which we will review the Matter and explain its terms to you. Upon completion of the Matter, the Firm will no longer be your representative. Any future services will require a separate retainer agreement.

The Firm's fee for this service shall be $750.00.

By executing this agreement, you acknowledge that there is uncertainty concerning the outcome of this matter and that the Firm and the undersigned representatives have made no guarantees as to the disposition of any phase of this matter. All representations and expression relative to the outcome of this matter, are only expressions of the said representative's opinions and do not constitute guarantees.

AGREED AND ACCEPTED

_____   _____
Client Name   Date

_____   _____
Rep's Name   Date

Retainer Agreement – Case Analysis

Via Email

July 1, 2021

Client Names
Client Address
City, State and Zip

RE: Fee Agreement for Representation for the Limited Purpose

Dear Taxpayer:

You have requested and _____ LLC (the "Firm") has agreed to represent you with regard to the following legal service(s) only:

To provide an analysis of your current tax situation and provide recommendations on the various options available to you (the "Matter")

The scope of the Firm's representation of you will consist of the Matter, as described above at which we will review the Matter and explain its terms to you. Upon completion of the Matter, the Firm will no longer be your representative. Any future services will require a separate retainer agreement.

The Firm's fee for this service shall be $1,500.00.

By executing this agreement, you acknowledge that there is uncertainty concerning the outcome of this matter and that the Firm and the undersigned representatives have made no guarantees as to the disposition of any phase of this matter. All representations and expression relative to the outcome of this matter, are only expressions of the said representative's opinions and do not constitute guarantees.

AGREED AND ACCEPTED

_____   _____
Client Name   Date

_____   _____
Rep's Name   Date

Sample Pricing Structure

- Consultation and Transcript Analysis: $1,500
- Streamlined Installment Agreement: $1,500
- Regular Installment Agreement/PPIA: $3,500 Retainer
- Offer-in-Compromise: $5,000 flat
- Offer appeal: $2,500 retainer
- Innocent Spouse: $5,000 retainer
- Innocent Spouse appeal: $2,500
- DATL/Audit Reconsideration: $2,500 (plus all exam work)
- IRS Exam: $5,000 retainer
- Penalty Abatement: $3,500 retainer

Retainers are all for work that is billed hourly due to the inability to know in advance how much work will be involved.

Other Important Practice Forms

Form 911 – Request for TAS Assistance

Form 911 (January 2022)

Department of the Treasury - Internal Revenue Service

Request for Taxpayer Advocate Service Assistance
(And Application for Taxpayer Assistance Order)

OMB Number 1545-1504

Section I – Taxpayer Information
(See Pages 3 and 4 for Form 911 Filing Requirements and Instructions for Completing this Form.)

1a. Taxpayer name as shown on tax return

1b. Taxpayer Identifying Number *(SSN, ITIN, EIN)*

2a. Spouse's name as shown on tax return *(if joint return)*

2b. Spouse's Taxpayer Identifying Number *(SSN, ITIN)*

3a. Taxpayer current street address *(number, street, & apt. number)*

3b. City

3c. State *(or foreign country)*

3d. ZIP code

4. Fax number *(if applicable)*

5. Email address

6. Person to contact if no authorized representative

7a. Daytime phone number

☐ Check if Cell Phone

7b. ☐ Check here if you consent to have confidential information about your tax issue left on your answering machine or voice message at this number.

8. Best time to call

9. Preferred language *(if applicable)*
   - ☐ TTY/TDD Line
   - ☐ Interpreter needed - Specify language other than English *(including sign language)*
   - ☐ Other *(specify)*

10. Tax form number *(1040, 941, 720, etc.)*

11. Tax year(s) or period(s)

12a. Describe the tax issue you are experiencing and any difficulties it may be creating
(If more space is needed, attach additional sheets.) (See instructions for completing Lines 12a and 12b)

12b. Describe the relief/assistance you are requesting *(if more space is needed, attach additional sheets)*

I understand that Taxpayer Advocate Service employees may contact third parties in order to respond to this request and I authorize such contacts to be made. Further, by authorizing the Taxpayer Advocate Service to contact third parties, I understand that I will not receive notice, pursuant to section 7602(c) of the Internal Revenue Code, of third parties contacted in connection with this request.

13a. Signature of taxpayer or corporate officer, and title, if applicable

13b. Date signed

14a. Signature of spouse *(if joint assistance request)*

14b. Date signed

Section II – Representative Information
(Attach Form 2848 if not already on file with the IRS.)

1. Name of authorized representative

2. Centralized Authorization File (CAF) number

3. Current mailing address

4. Daytime phone number

☐ Check if Cell Phone

5. Fax number

6. Signature of representative

7. Date signed

Catalog Number 16965S   www.irs.gov   Form **911** (Rev. 1-2022)

Page 2

Section III – Initiating Employee Information *(Section III is to be completed by the IRS only)*

Taxpayer name			Taxpayer Identifying Number *(TIN)*	
1. Name of employee	2. Phone number	3a. Function	3b. Operating division	4. Organization code no.

5. How identified and received *(check the appropriate box)* | 6. IRS received date

IRS function identified issue as meeting Taxpayer Advocate Service (TAS) criteria
- ☐ (r) Functional referral *(function identified taxpayer issue as meeting TAS criteria)*
- ☐ (x) Congressional correspondence/inquiry not addressed to TAS but referred for TAS handling
  Name of senator/representative _____

Taxpayer or representative requested TAS assistance
- ☐ (n) Taxpayer or representative called into a National Taxpayer Advocate (NTA) toll-free site
- ☐ (s) Functional referral *(taxpayer or representative specifically requested TAS assistance)*

7. TAS criteria *(Check the appropriate box. NOTE: Checkbox 9 is for TAS Use Only)*
- ☐ (1) The taxpayer is experiencing economic harm or is about to suffer economic harm.
- ☐ (2) The taxpayer is facing an immediate threat of adverse action.
- ☐ (3) The taxpayer will incur significant costs if relief is not granted (including fees for professional representation).
- ☐ (4) The taxpayer will suffer irreparable injury or long-term adverse impact if relief is not granted.

(if any items 1-4 are checked, complete Question 9 below)

- ☐ (5) The taxpayer has experienced a delay of more than 30 days to resolve a tax account problem.
- ☐ (6) The taxpayer did not receive a response or resolution to their problem or inquiry by the date promised.
- ☐ (7) A system or procedure has either failed to operate as intended or failed to resolve the taxpayer's problem or dispute within the IRS.
- ☐ (8) The manner in which the tax laws are being administered raise considerations of equity or have impaired or will impair the taxpayer's rights.
- ☐ (9) The NTA determines compelling public policy warrants assistance to an individual or group of taxpayers **(TAS Use Only)**

8. What action(s) did you take to help resolve the issue? *(This block MUST be completed by the initiating employee)*
If you were unable to resolve the issue, state the reason why (if applicable)

9. Provide a description of the Taxpayer's situation, and where appropriate, explain the circumstances that are creating the economic burden and how the Taxpayer could be adversely affected if the requested assistance is not provided
(This block MUST be completed by the initiating employee)

10. How did the taxpayer learn about the Taxpayer Advocate Service
- ☐ IRS forms or publications   ☐ Media   ☐ IRS employee   ☐ Other *(specify)* _____

Catalog Number 16965S   www.irs.gov   Form **911** (Rev. 1-2022)

Page 3

Instructions for completing Form 911

Important Things You Should Know

- Remember to furnish any documentation you believe would assist us in resolving the issue, as this may result in a quicker resolution of your issue.
- You can expect a Taxpayer Advocate Service employee to attempt call you to discuss your Form 911. If unable to reach you by phone, we will mail you a letter.
- If you are a low-income taxpayer who needs help in resolving a tax dispute with the Internal Revenue Service and cannot afford representation, you may qualify for free or low-cost assistance from a Low Income Taxpayer Clinic (LITC). For more information, see Publication 4134 or visit our LITC page at: https://www.taxpayeradvocate.irs.gov/about-us/low-income-taxpayer-clinics-litc/.

Form 911 Filing Requirements

The Taxpayer Advocate Service (TAS) is an independent organization within the Internal Revenue Service (IRS) that helps taxpayers and protects taxpayers' rights. We can offer you help if your tax problem is causing a financial difficulty, you've tried and been unable to resolve your issue with the IRS, or you believe an IRS system, process, or procedure just isn't working as it should. If you qualify for our assistance, which is always free, we will do everything possible to help you. Visit www.taxpayeradvocate.irs.gov or call 877-777-4778.

Where to Send this Form:

- **The quickest method is Fax.** TAS has at least one office in every state, the District of Columbia, and Puerto Rico. Submit this request to the TAS office in your geographic area. You can find the fax number in the government listings in your local telephone directory, on our website at www.taxpayeradvocate.irs.gov/contact-us/submit-a-request-for-assistance/, or in Publication 1546, *Taxpayer Advocate Service - Your Voice at the IRS*, Local Offices by State and Location on p. 11.
- **You also can mail this form.** You can find the mailing address and phone number (voice) of your local Taxpayer Advocate office in your phone book, on our website, and in Pub. 1546, or get this information by calling our toll-free number: 1-877-777-4778.

  Note: If you are you sending the form from overseas, use Fax number: 1-304-707-9793 (Not a toll-free number for U.S. taxpayers) or mail it to: Taxpayer Advocate Service, Internal Revenue Service, PO Box 11996, San Juan, Puerto Rico 00922.
- Be sure to fill out the form completely and submit it to the TAS office nearest you so we can work your issue as soon as possible.

What Happens Next?

If you don't receive a response within 30 days of submitting Form 911, call 877-777-4778 for assistance.

Important Notes: Please be aware that by submitting this form, you are authorizing TAS to contact third parties as necessary to respond to your request, and you may not receive further notice about these contacts. For more information see IRC 7602(c).

Caution: TAS will not consider frivolous arguments raised on this form. You can find examples of frivolous arguments in Publication 2105, Why do I have to Pay Taxes? If you use this form to raise frivolous arguments, you may be subject to a penalty of $5,000, in addition to any other penalty provided by law.

Paperwork Reduction Act Notice: We ask for the information on this form to carry out the Internal Revenue laws of the United States. Your response is voluntary. You are not required to provide the information requested on a form that is subject to the Paperwork Reduction Act unless the form displays a valid OMB control number. Books or records relating to a form or its instructions must be retained as long as their contents may become material in the administration of any Internal Revenue law. Generally, tax returns and return information are confidential, as required by Code section 6103. Although the time needed to complete this form may vary depending on individual circumstances, the estimated average time is 30 minutes.

Should you have comments concerning the accuracy of this time estimate or suggestions for making this form simpler, please write to: **Internal Revenue Service**, Tax Products Coordinating Committee, Room 6406, 1111 Constitution Ave. NW, Washington, DC 20224.

Instructions for Section I

1a.	Enter the taxpayer's name as shown on the tax return that relates to this request for assistance.
1b.	Enter your Taxpayer Identifying Number. If you're an individual this will be either a Social Security Number (SSN) or Individual Taxpayer Identification Number (ITIN). If you're a business entity this will be your Employer Identification Number (EIN) *(e.g. a partnership, corporation, trust or self-employed individual with employees)*.
2a.	Enter your spouse's name *(if applicable)* if this request relates to a jointly filed return.
2b.	Enter your spouse's Taxpayer Identifying Number *(SSN or ITIN)* if this request relates to a jointly filed return.
3a-d.	Enter your current mailing address, including street number and name, city, state, or foreign country, and zip code.
4.	Enter your fax number, including the area code.
5.	Enter your email address. TAS may use email to receive and share information with you about your case, but only after discussing the use of email with you and obtaining your consent.

Instructions for Section I continue on the next page

Catalog Number 16965S www.irs.gov Form **911** (Rev. 1-2022)

Page 4

Instructions for Section I - *(Continued from Page 3)*

6. Enter the name of the individual we should contact if Section II is not being used. For partnerships, corporations, trusts, etc., enter the name of the individual authorized to act on the entity's behalf. If the contact person is not the taxpayer or other authorized individual, please see the Instructions for Section II.

7a. Enter your daytime telephone number, including the area code. If this is a cell phone number, please check the box.

7b. If you have an answering machine or voice mail at this number and you consent to TAS leaving confidential information about your tax issue at this number, please check the box. You are not obligated to have information about your tax issue left at this number. If other individuals have access to the answering machine or the voice mail and you do not wish for them to receive any confidential information about your tax issue, please do not check the box.

8. Indicate the best time to call you. Please specify A.M. or P.M. hours.

9. Indicate any special communication needs *(such as sign language)*. Specify any language other than English.

10. Enter the number of the Federal tax return or form that relates to this request. For example, an individual taxpayer with an income tax issue would enter Form 1040.

11. Enter the quarterly, annual, or other tax year or period that relates to this request. For example, if this request involves an income tax issue, enter the calendar or fiscal year, if an employment tax issue, enter the calendar quarter.

12a. Describe the tax issue you are experiencing and any difficulties it may be creating. Specify the actions that the IRS has taken (or not taken) to resolve the issue. If the issue involves an IRS delay of more than 30 days in resolving your issue, indicate the date you first contacted the IRS for assistance. See Section III for a specific list of TAS criteria. For further information on the services TAS provides, see Publication 1546, Taxpayer Advocate Service - Your Voice at the IRS, available at https://www.irs.gov/pub/irs-pdf/p1546.pdf.

12b. Describe the relief/assistance you are requesting. Specify the action you want taken and believe necessary to resolve the issue. Furnish any documentation you believe would assist us in resolving the issue.

13-14. If this is a joint assistance request, both spouses must sign and date the request. If only one spouse is requesting assistance, only that spouse must sign the request. If this request is being submitted for another individual, only a person authorized and empowered to act on that individual's behalf should sign the request. Requests for corporations must be signed by an officer and include the officer's title.

Note: The signing of this request allows the IRS by law to suspend any applicable statutory periods of limitation relating to the assessment or collection of taxes. However, it does not suspend any applicable periods for you to perform acts related to assessment or collection, such as petitioning the Tax Court for redetermination of a deficiency or requesting a Collection Due Process hearing.

Instructions for Section II

Taxpayers: If you wish to have a representative act on your behalf, you must give him/her power of attorney or tax information authorization for the tax return(s) and period(s) involved. For additional information see Form 2848, Power of Attorney and Declaration of Representative, or Form 8821, Tax Information Authorization, and the accompanying instructions.

Representatives: If you are an authorized representative submitting this request on behalf of the taxpayer identified in Section I, complete Blocks 1 through 7 of Section II. Attach a copy of Form 2848, Form 8821, or other power of attorney. Enter your Centralized Authorization File (CAF) number in Block 2 of Section II. The CAF number is the unique number that the IRS assigns to a representative after Form 2848 or Form 8821 is filed with an IRS office.

Note: Form 8821 does not authorize your appointee to advocate your position with respect to the Federal tax laws; to execute waivers, consents, or closing agreements; or to otherwise represent you before the IRS. Form 8821 does authorize anyone you designate to inspect and/or receive your confidential tax information in any office of the IRS, for the type of tax and tax periods you list on Form 8821.

Instructions for Section III **(For IRS Use Only)** *Please complete this section in its entirety.*

Enter the taxpayer's name and taxpayer identifying number from the first page of this form.

1-5. Enter your name, phone number, Function (*e.g., ACS, Collection, Examination, Customer Service, etc.*), Operating Division (*W&I, SB/SE, LB&I, or TE/GE*), the Organization code number for your office (*e.g., 18 for AUSC, 95 for Los Angeles*), and Check the appropriate box that best reflects how the need for TAS assistance was identified. Enter the date the taxpayer or representative called or visited an IRS office to request TAS assistance. Or enter the date when the IRS received the Congressional correspondence/inquiry or a written request for TAS assistance from the taxpayer or representative. If the IRS identified the taxpayer's issue as meeting TAS criteria, enter the date this determination was made.

6. Check the box that best describes the reason TAS assistance is requested. Box 9 is for TAS Use Only.

7. State the action(s) you took to help resolve the taxpayer's issue. State the reason(s) that prevented you from resolving the taxpayer's issue. For example, levy proceeds cannot be returned because they were already applied to a valid liability; an overpayment cannot be refunded because the statutory period for issuing a refund expired; or current law precludes a specific interest abatement.

8. Provide a description of the taxpayer's situation, and where appropriate, explain the circumstances that are creating the economic burden and how the taxpayer could be adversely affected if the requested assistance is not provided.

9. Ask the taxpayer how he or she learned about the TAS and indicate the response here.

Catalog Number 16965S   www.irs.gov   Form **911** (Rev. 1-2022)

FOIA Request – Admin File for Income Taxes

February 28, 2020

<u>VIA FAX: 877-891-6035</u>
Internal Revenue Service
GLDS Support Services
Stop 93A
Post Office Box 621506
Atlanta, GA 30362

    Re: **Taxpayer:**
            Current Address:
            Taxpayer ID No.:

Dear Sir or Madam:

This is a request under the Freedom of Information Act.

5. **Name and Address**

    Requestor:

    Clients:

6. **Description of the Requested Records**

    The undersigned is the representative to _____. We respectfully request copies of the taxpayer's administrative file for tax years _____.

7. **Proof of Identity**

    As proof of identity, I am including a photocopy of my driver's license and a copy of my Power of Attorney and Declaration of Representative (Form 2848).

8. **Commitment to Pay Any Fees Which May Apply**

    The undersigned is willing to pay for fees associated with this request. If the request shall exceed $100, the undersigned requests to be notified.

6. **Compelling Need for Speedy Response**

    The Taxpayer is in the process of appealing the imposition of penalties related to the failure to file certain foreign reporting forms and the files are necessary to do so.

I declare that the above stated information is true and accurate to the best of my knowledge under the penalty of perjury.

Please call me with any questions.

Very truly yours,

TAX PRO NAME

Request for Decertification for Passport Renewal

February 28, 2020

<u>VIA CERTIFIED MAIL</u>
Department of the Treasury
Internal Revenue Service
Attn: Passport
P.O. Box 8208
Philadelphia, PA 19101-8208

  Re: **Decertification of Taxpayer, SSN _____**

Dear Sir or Madam,

The above referenced taxpayer received your letter 508C informing him that the IRS would send his name to the Department of State to have his passport revoked. A copy of that letter is attached, along with a copy of my Form 2848.

The Taxpayer has since received word that his request for an installment agreement was accepted, a copy of that letter is also attached.

We are requesting he be de-certified with the Department of State so that he may renew his passport.

If you have any questions or concerns, please feel free to contact me at (203) XXX-XXXX.

Very truly yours,

TAX PRO NAME

Enclosures

C. Taxpayer

Power of Attorney – Revoke

February 28, 2020

<u>VIA FAX</u>
Internal Revenue Service
CAF Unit (MAMC)
5333 Getwell Rd
Stop 8423
Memphis, TN 38118

    Re: **Client's Name**

Dear Sir or Madam,

Our office no longer represents Client's name. Please withdraw the Power of Attorney for myself.

Please contact the taxpayer directly from this point forward.

Very truly yours,

TAX PRO NAME

Transcript Monitoring Agreement

February 28, 2020

CLIENT'S NAME
CLIENT'S ADDRESS

Re: Case Closing/Ongoing Monitoring

Dear CLIENT NAME,

Our normal process for IRS cases is to close our file when the case is over and revoke our Power-of-Attorney ("POA"). However, we find clients often want us to maintain our POA and continue monitoring their transcripts through our system, alerting you when anything shows up on the transcripts, so you have advanced notice of an IRS adjustment, you have been flagged for an audit, or there is a collection issue.

We generally charge an annual fee of $500 to update the POA and monitor the IRS Transcript system.

If you would like us to do this for you, please sign and date below. We will send you an updated POA we will then file and use to monitor the IRS system and receive any notices. If you choose not to do this, or we do not hear back from you in 14 days, we will go ahead and revoke our POA and close your file.

Thank you,

Please sign and date below if you want us to maintain the POA and monitor your IRS account.

_____   _____
Clients name   Date

Tax Information Release

CONSENT AND AUTHORIZATION FORM
RELEASE/EXCHANGE OF CLIENT INFORMATION

Client Name: _____("Client")

SSN/EIN: _____

If Client is not an individual, name of authorized representative:

_____

Title: _____

Client has asked us to provide tax information to a third party. Federal law prohibits us from doing so without your written consent. If you wish for us to provide your tax information to a third party you must complete and sign this form. Please note as follows:

1. Federal law requires that you provide us with explicit direction to release your tax information to a third party.
2. Unless authorized by law, we cannot disclose, without your consent, your tax return and other financial information to third parties.
3. If you consent to the disclosure of your tax return information, Federal law may not protect your tax return and other financial information from further use or distribution.
4. If you do not specify the duration of your consent, your consent is valid for one year.
5. You are not required to complete this form. If we obtain your signature on this form by conditioning our services on your consent, your consent will not be valid.

I authorize the release of all financial and tax information to the below name Recipient for the following years _____. This information will include, but is not limited to, financial and accounting reports, income tax returns, bank statements, wage statements, and other confidential documents.

I do not authorize the following items or companies to be included in this authorization (leave blank if no restrictions):

_____

Please release my information to (must be completed):

Name of third party to whom you want your tax information released:

_____ ("Recipient")

Name of authorized individual at Recipient to whom you authorize the tax information to be released:

_____

_____

Address, Phone Number, and Email Address of Recipient:

_____

Client Signature: _____   Date:_____

Witness: _____   Date:_____

Name: _____

Payroll Tax Issues

Payroll Tax Document Checklist

{Please provide us all that apply}

Tax Returns:

- Last three years of tax returns

IRS Notices:

- Copies of any IRS notices, especially if received via certified mail

Assets:

- Bank Accounts
    - Last six months of bank statements for all accounts
- Investments
    - Most recent statement for all investment accounts (Stocks, Mutual Funds, Trading Accounts)
    - Most recent statement for all retirement accounts (IRA, 401(k), 403(b), etc)
    - Copies of all 401(k) and 403(b) plan documents
    - Statements of value for all other investments, including documentation of loans against any investment
- Virtual Currency (Bitcoin)
    - Recent statement of any virtual currency you have, the amount and its current value
- Foreign Assets, trusts or bank accounts
    - Last 6 months of statements on all accounts
- Life Insurance
    - Statement showing the premium and cash value of life insurance
- Real Estate
    - Printouts for the value of any real estate owned (appraisal, Zillow, etc)
    - Recent mortgage statements for any property owned

- Recent statement for credit lines/home equity loans secured by any real estate
- Automobiles
  - Kelly Blue Book printouts for value of each vehicle
  - Recent monthly statement of any loan balance and monthly payment
  - Recent monthly statement showing the lease payment and time remaining on the lease
- Collectables (artwork, jewelry, collections, etc)
  - Statement of value or appraisal for collectables
  - Copy of your homeowners or renter's insurance including riders.

Income & Expenses:

- We need your current income for you and your spouse/partner/significant other you reside with/anyone who contributes to the household income (whether they are responsible or not). Please get us any of the following if they apply:
  - A current profit and loss for each business or rental activity
  - If you or your spouse are wage earners, your three most recent pay stubs
  - Proof of any social security income
  - Proof of annuity or retirement income
  - Proof of any child support or alimony received
  - Proof of any other income or cash flow stream into the household
- Last three months of utility bills
- Proof of your mortgage payment and balance. If you rent, we need your current lease agreement
- Proof of monthly car payments, whether loan or lease, with the balance remaining
- Proof of health insurance and premium amount
- Proof of life insurance premiums
- Proof of disability insurance premiums
- Proof of any alimony or child support you or your spouse pay, including the divorce or separation agreement and court order

- Home equity statement
- Proof of any judgments and payment plans to secured creditors
- Proof of any payment plans with state taxing authorities
- Proof of student loan balances and payments
- Proof of current estimated tax payments (unless you are a wage earner, in which case they are reflected on your paystubs)
- Proof of out-of-pocket healthcare expenses, IF they exceed $52/per person per month (or $114/month for anyone 65 or older)
- Proof of child/dependent care expense, such as daycare and after-school programs
- Proof of any other necessary expenses, such as mandatory union dues, restitution payments, etc.

FOIA Request – for Trust Fund Administrative File

February 28, 2020

<u>VIA FAX</u>
IRS FOIA Request
HQ FOIA
Stop 211
PO Box 621506
Atlanta, GA 30362-3006

      Re: **Taxpayer:** _____
            Current Address: _____
            SSN: _____

This is a request under the Freedom of Information Act.

1. **Name and Address**

    Requestor:

    Representative's Name

    Reps Street Address

    Rep City, State and Zip

    Client:

    Taxpayer's Name

    Taxpayer's Street Address

    Taxpayer's City, State and Zip

2. **Description of the Requested Records**

    The undersigned represents TAXPAYER NAME (the "Requestor"). We respectfully request copies of the taxpayers' administrative file regarding his civil penalties under IRC § 6672 for the quarters 6/30/2015 through and including 12/31/2016.

3. **Proof of Identity**

    As proof of identity, I am including a photocopy of my driver's license and a copy of my Power of Attorney and Declaration of Representative (Form 2848).

4. **Commitment to Pay Any Fees Which May Apply**

   The undersigned is willing to pay for fees associated with this request. If the request shall exceed $100, the undersigned requests to be notified

5. **Compelling Need for Speedy Response**

   We are in the middle of an Appeal of these civil penalties and require the information to properly present our case.

I declare that the above stated information is true and accurate to the best of my knowledge under the penalty of perjury.

Please call me with any questions.

Very truly yours,

TAX PRO NAME

Protest of Proposed Trust Fund Assessment

February 28, 2020

<u>VIA FAX</u>
Internal Revenue Service
ATTN: _____
Street Address
City, State Zip

      Re: Taxpayer: _____
             Current Address: _____
             SSN: _____

Dear Sir or Madam,

My power of attorney (Form 2848) to represent the taxpayer in this matter is included.

Reference is made to the September ____, 2018 letter that proposed an assessment for unpaid trust funds in regard to the above named taxpayer for _____ Inc., a copy of which is attached. This is to protest the proposed assessment and to request a conference with the Appeals Division. The following information is submitted in support of this appeal.

I.   CONFERENCE

The taxpayer wants to appeal the determination of the Internal Revenue Service and requests a hearing before the Regional Office of Appeals in the East Hartford, Connecticut Appeals office.

II.   NAME AND ADDRESS

      Taxpayer Name
      Street Address
      City, State Zip
      SSN: _____

III. DATE AND SYMBOLS FROM LETTER

September 20, 2018

Letter 1153 (DO)(Rev. 3-2002)

IV. TAX PERIODS

12/31/2008

03/31/2009

V. ITEMIZED SCHEDULE OF APPEAL ITEMS

The determination that the taxpayer is a responsible person as defined in IRC § 6672 for the unpaid trust funds for the tax periods listed above in the amount of $296,096.67.

VI. STATEMENT OF FACTS

The taxpayer worked as Vice President of Operations at _____, Inc., ("NAME"). The NAME was in the construction business, and the taxpayer was responsible for managing the job site operations under the general supervision and direction of _____. The taxpayer's specific duties included supervising of all job personnel, reviewing of job budgets, scheduling, attending job meetings, and consulting with the Company's agents and employees as required.

Mr. NAME was responsible for the finances. Mr. NAME ran operations in the office, and only he signed payroll checks and other documents as the sole shareholder. The taxpayer was given an officer's title, but he had no financial responsibilities in the Companies. The taxpayer was given signature rights but in ten years never signed a single check, legal document, or tax document. A stamp of his signature was made, but to his knowledge the stamp was never used. Ms. _____, who was in charge of payroll function for the years of 1983 to 2007, affirms that the taxpayer had nothing to do with nor signed a single check. A copy of her affidavit is attached.

VII. LAW AND AUTHORITIES

The issue is whether the taxpayer meets the definition of a "responsible person" who willfully failed to have the payroll taxes paid over to the government IRC § 6672.

> IRC § 6672 states the following:
>
> Any person required to collect, truthfully account for, and pay over any tax imposed by this title who willfully fails to collect such tax, or truthfully account for and pay over such tax, or willfully attempts in any manner to evade or defeat any such tax or the payment thereof, shall, in addition to other penalties provided by law, be liable to a penalty equal to the total amount of the tax evaded, or not collected, or not accounted for and paid over.

In other words, pursuant to IRC § 6672 and Regulation § 301.6672-1, the Trust Fund Recovery penalty is only imposed on individuals who:

1. Were required to collect, account for, and pay over the taxes, and
2. Willfully failed to do so.

Based upon the foregoing, the taxpayer, though an officer with authority, lacked the functional responsibility for the payroll taxes of the Companies. He was never involved with the payroll function and in 10 years never signed a check or return for the Companies. It was not until after the taxpayer left the Companies that he learned from the government that taxes were owed. Prior to that he had no knowledge nor access to the financial information of the company and was never made aware by anyone that the company had failed to pay its payroll taxes or even had a money issue. Given that the taxpayer was never involved in the Companies' taxes and did not have knowledge of the payroll tax problem, he therefore lacked the requisite willfulness required under IRC § 6672. The taxpayer therefore should not be held responsible for the companies unpaid payroll taxes.

This protest was prepared by the undersigned based upon direct involvement of TAXPAYER. To the best of my knowledge and understanding all of the statements of facts contained in the protest are true and correct.

Very truly yours,

TAX PRO NAME

Enclosures

C: Taxpayer

Sample Affidavit

State of Connecticut)

) ss. _____

County of New Haven)

AFFIDAVIT

I, _____, of New Haven, Connecticut hereby aver as follows:

1. That I am over eighteen years of age and believe in the obligations of an oath;
2. I was an employee of _____, Inc. ("Company") during the period of 1984 through its dissolution in 2007.
3. My role was Supervisor in-charge of payroll for the Company.
4. During Mr. TAXPAYER's time as a Vice-President at the Company he never signed a payroll check.
5. Mr. TAXPAYER never signed any tax returns or payroll-related documents
6. Mr. TAXPAYER was not involved in the payroll process at all.
7. The only person who signed payroll checks and determined which vendors to pay and not pay during my time with the company was the owner, Mr. _____.
8. I am aware this affidavit is being submitted to the Internal Revenue Service for their consideration of a material tax matter.

Subscribed and sworn to, under penalty of perjury, this ____ day of November, 2018.

_____
WITNESSES NAME

Dated at _____, Connecticut, this _____ day of November, 2018.

_____
Notary Public

Letter – Voluntary Payment Designated Against the Trust Fund Assessment

February 28, 2020

<u>VIA FEDERAL EXPRESS</u>
Department of Treasury
Internal Revenue Service
Attn: REVENUE OFFICER NAME
Street Address
City, State Zip

    Re: **TAXPAYER NAME, SSN: xxx-xx-xxxx**
             Directed Payment of Trust Fund Portion of Employment Taxes
             Employer: COMPANY NAME, Inc., EIN XX-XXXXXXX

Dear REVENUE OFFICER NAME:

This office represents TAXPAYERS NAME and COMPANY NAME, Inc. Enclosed please find a check in the amount of $499,261.57 (check # _____) payable to the U.S. Treasury. Pursuant to Rev. Proc. 2002-26, 2002-15 IRB 746, 2002-1 CB 746 and IRM 5.1.2.3 and 26 C.F.R. 301.7701-2(c)(2)(iv), this payment constitutes a voluntary payment and should be applied to reduce any trust fund recovery penalty and/or trust fund portions of employment taxes for which TAXPAYERS NAME is personally liable.

If for any reason the Internal Revenue Service intends and/or expects to apply the enclosed payment not in accordance with this letter of direction, the U.S. Treasury is not authorized to deposit the enclosed check and it should be returned to me.

Please call me should you have any questions.

Very truly yours,

TAX PRO NAME

Sample Refund Complaint

UNITED STATES DISTRICT COURT
DISTRICT OF CONNECTICUT

TAXPAYER	:	CIVIL ACTION NO.
Plaintiff	:	
v.	:	
UNITED STATES OF AMERICA	:	
Defendant	:	APRIL 1, 20__

COMPLAINT AND JURY DEMAND

The plaintiff, TAXPAYER NAME (the "Plaintiff"), hereby brings the following complaint upon information and belief as follows:

PARTIES

1. The plaintiff, TAXPAYER NAME (the "Plaintiff"), is a resident of the State of Connecticut with a place of residence at STREET, CITY, CT 06___.

2. The defendant, United States of America ("USA"), is the proper party in interest for seeking refund of monies paid to the Internal Revenue Service (the "IRS").

JURISDICTION AND VENUE

3. This Court has subject matter jurisdiction over this matter pursuant to 28 U.S.C. § 1346(a)(1), 26 U.S.C. §§ 6532(a), 6672(d), 7402 and 7422.

4. This Court has personal jurisdiction and venue over this matter as the Plaintiff is a resident of the State of Connecticut. The USA is amenable to service of process pursuant to Fed. R. Civ. P. 4(i).

COUNT ONE: Claim for Refund Pursuant to 26 U.S.C. § 7422

1-4. The Plaintiff incorporates paragraphs 1 through 4 of the Complaint as the corresponding paragraphs to this Count as if fully stated herein.

5. For many years NAME OF CORPORATION, Inc. ("CORP"), was a successful electrical contracting firm.

6. At all times relevant hereto, BOOKEEPER NAME ("BOOKKEEPER"), was a resident of the State of Connecticut with a last known place of address at 33 Lindale Street # 89, Stamford CT 06902. Until June 2008 BOOKKEEPER was employed by CORP as its bookkeeper.

7. At all times relevant hereto, the defendant, DEFANDANT ("DEFENDANT"), was a resident of the State of Connecticut with a last known place of address at 64 West Hill Circle, Stamford CT 06902. DEFENDANT was a fifty (50%) owner of CORP and the corporate treasurer.

8. CORP is owned fifty (50%) percent each by the Plaintiff and DEFENDANT.

9. During the construction and housing boom of 2002-2007, CORP's work load grew significantly and, as such, retained additional employees and expanded its operations.

10. Most of CORP's employees were union members.

11. During the second half of 2007 CORP began to experience issues with on-going projects, including increased material costs and increased default rates by its customers.

12. During the beginning of 2008 the Plaintiff injected more than $140,000.00 of his personal funds into CORP to ensure bills, including federal tax payments, were paid.

13. However, unbeknownst to the Plaintiff, CORP's bookkeeper, BOOKKEEPER, failed to make employment tax deposits even though he was specifically instructed to do so, and reminded on a weekly basis, by the Plaintiff.

14. During all times relevant hereto, every Monday morning the Plaintiff questioned BOOKKEEPER as to whether the tax deposit payment concerning the prior

week's payroll had been made. BOOKKEEPER always acknowledge the reminders and indicated that appropriate tax deposits were being made to the IRS.

15. Despite the repeated admonitions by the Plaintiff to BOOKKEEPER', and BOOKKEEPER assurances that he was making federal tax deposits, BOOKKEEPER in fact failed to actually make the tax deposits.

16. Indeed, during the times relevant hereto, the Plaintiff had invested and/or lent his own personal funds to CORP to ensure that CORP had sufficient cash on hand to make federal tax deposits. Thus, despite BOOKKEEPER' explicit instruction from the Plaintiff and his assurances that federal tax deposits were being made, BOOKKEEPER redirected the funds injected into CORP by the Plaintiff for other purposes for which it was not intended.

17. On account of, inter alia, BOOKKEEPER' conduct filed for Chapter 11 bankruptcy on June 6, 2008.

18. On or about December 15, 2008, REVENUE OFFICER'S NAME, Revenue Officer, issued a proposed assessment of a Trust Fund Recovery Penalty pursuant to 26 U.S.C. § 6672 against the Plaintiff for the first quarter and second quarter of 2008. (A copy of the Proposed Assessment is attached hereto as Exhibit A.)

19. The Plaintiff timely appealed the proposed assessment, which was denied, and the proposed assessment became final in the amount of: (a) $69,471.09, Assessed Balance for March 31, 2008; and (b) $54,718.32, Assessed Balance for June 30, 2008 for a total of $124,189.41 (the "Trust Fund Recovery Penalty Assessment"), plus accrued interest.

20. On October 14, 2009 the Plaintiff paid a portion of the tax due for each assessed period and requested a refund thereon. See, Steele v. United States, 280 F.2d 89 (8th Cir. 1960); IRM 5.7.6.6 (2). A copy of the payments made to the IRS and Refund Requests are attached hereto as Exhibit B.

21. On March 3, 2010 said refund requests were denied. A copy of the denial letter is attached hereto as Exhibit C.

22. Pursuant to 26 U.S.C. § 6672, Congress has only authorized the IRS to assess and collect a "trust fund recovery penalty" against taxpayers who are both "responsible persons" and who "willfully" failed to collect, account for and pay over the "trust fund" taxes of a corporate employer.

23. At all times relevant in this matter, from January through April 2008, the Plaintiff did not act "willfully" as that terms is defined by 26 U.S.C. § 6672.

24. The IRS' assessment of the Trust Fund Recovery Penalty Assessment against the Plaintiff was improper, excessive, erroneous and illegal.

25. The Plaintiff is entitled to a refund of all payments made to the USA on account of the IRS' improper assessment of a Trust Fund Recovery Penalty Assessment. Further, the Plaintiff is entitled to a determination that he is not liable for the Trust Fund Recovery Penalty Assessment against him.

WHEREFORE the Plaintiff prays that the following relief enter:

1. A declaration that he is not liable for the Trust Fund Recovery Penalty assessed against him;

2. A declaration and/or injunction prohibiting the IRS from enforcing and/or collecting the Trust Fund Recovery Penalty assessed against him;

3. Refund of amounts paid on account of said Trust Fund Recovery Penalty;

4. Attorneys fees and costs; and

5. Such other relief as the court may deem just and proper.

THE PLAINTIFF: TAXPAYER'S NAME

By: _____

THE PLAINTIFF DEMANDS TRIAL BY JURY

Penalty Abatement

Abatement Request – Bad Accountant

February 28, 2020

<u>VIA FAX</u>
Internal Revenue Service
Address Block
Address Block

    Re: TAXPAYER NAME (eg. Fred Flintstone and Wilma Flintstone)

Dear Sir or Madam:

Please accept this letter in furtherance of the taxpayers', Fred Flintstone and Wilma Flintstone ("Taxpayers") Form 843 Claim for Refund and Request for Abatement for request for abatement of all penalties and interest associated with accuracy and failure to pay taxes due for 2013-2016 tax years.

The Taxpayers have had a long history of payment compliance prior to issues that arose with their former accountant, which caused the instant issues.

The Taxpayer's former accountant, Bedrock Accounting, Inc. ("Bedrock"), provided services for the Taxpayers individually and for the Taxpayer's companies, Wabba Dabbaa ("Wabba") and Doo, Inc. ("Doo") between 2012 and 2016. According to Bedrock's website, Bedrock brings "over 45 years experience to the small business owner who is faced with decreasing profitability, increasing taxes, tax notices/surprises, or simply wanting more time."

The Taxpayers entrusted Bedrock to provide accounting services and prepare and file their individual tax returns in addition to Wabba and Doo's business income return. During the period at issue, the Taxpayer had significant trouble reaching Bedrock for extended periods. Bedrock also provided tax advice to Wabba and Doo that the Taxpayers later found to have further harmed their tax situation.

After the Taxpayers became aware of the extent of their tax issues, the Taxpayers hired Barney Rubble, CPA ("Rubble") to prepare and file their individual tax returns and Wabba and Doo's tax returns. Rubble spent countless hours cleaning up Bedrock's mess so that the 2016 returns could be filed. However, unbeknownst to the Taxpayer,

Rubble was amidst a divorce and would be unable to see his case through to the end. Thus, the Taxpayers lost another professional that they hired to assist with its tax problems and further delayed the filing of the return. During this period, the Taxpayers entered into an installment agreement to attempt to repay their tax liability but with their accounting in such disrepair, they were unable to make the payments.

The Taxpayers hired a third accountant, Dino, LLC ("Dino"), to finally get their accounting back on track. Dino reviewed the work of Bedrock and identified several issues (see Exhibit A, Dino's letter to Taxpayer).

The Taxpayers' 2014 income tax return prepared by Bedrock was audited which led to a $81,090 liability as calculated in the Income Tax Examination Changes Line 11. The Taxpayers believe the correct tax liability is $49,993. The backup documentation is enclosed with Exhibit A, as provided by the Taxpayers' current accountant, Dino.

Since 2017, the Taxpayer has made every effort to the pay their taxes and maintain compliance. The Taxpayer's 2017 return was a refund. However, the Taxpayers have been left deep debt due to the poor accounting services of Bedrock. They have two mortgages on their home, both of which are near foreclosure. The State of Connecticut has levied them due to their state tax liability. They have virtually no assets and no savings for retirement (the Taxpayers are both in their late 50s).

Further, the Taxpayers, as a result of the tax lien that was placed on them, have been unable to properly run their business. They were unable to purchase a building for Wabba's body shop due to the tax lien.

The Taxpayers clearly had no intention of disobeying the taxing statutes – they hired what they thought were competent professionals to help them the moment they started their businesses. Penalties for late payment of tax and accuracy related penalties are governed by IRC §§ 6651 and 6662. In both sections, a taxpayer can have the penalties abated if it can establish that the failure to comply with the rules was due to reasonable cause and not due to intentional disregard. 26 C.F.R. § 301.6651-1(c)(1) states:

A failure to pay will be considered to be due to reasonable cause to the extent that the taxpayer has made a satisfactory showing that he exercised ordinary business care and prudence in providing for payment of his tax liability and was nevertheless either unable to pay the tax or would suffer an undue hardship (as described in Section 1.6161-1(b) of this chapter) if he paid on the due date. In determining whether the taxpayer was unable to pay the tax in spite of the exercise of ordinary business care and prudence in providing for payment of his tax liability, consideration will be given to all facts and circumstances of the taxpayer's financial situation, including the amount and nature of the taxpayer's expenditures in light of the income (or other amounts) he could, at the time of such expenditures, reasonably expect to receive prior to the date prescribed for the payment of the tax....

The term "undue hardship" is defined in 26 C.F.R. § 1.6161-1(b):

The term "undue hardship" means more than an inconvenience to the taxpayer. It must appear that substantial financial loss, for example, loss due to the sale of property at a sacrifice price, will result to the taxpayer for making payment on the due date of the amount with respect to which the extension is desired. If a market exists, the sale of property at the current market price is not ordinarily considered as resulting in an undue hardship.

The Internal Revenue Manual explains that the Service, when deciding on abatement in the first instance, should be equitable and penalties, in fact, exist to encourage voluntary compliance by supporting the standards of "behavior required by the Internal Revenue Code." IRM § 20.1.1.2. In this regard, penalties should:

1. Be severe enough to deter noncompliance.
2. Encourage noncompliant taxpayers to comply.
3. Be objectively proportioned to the offense.
4. Be used as an opportunity to educate taxpayers and encourage their future compliance.

IRM § 20.1.1.2.1(8). Penalties should also relate to the standards of behavior they encourage. In making a determination as to whether there is reasonable cause, the Internal Revenue Manual says that IRS will consider the following, among other factors:

- Whether the taxpayer's reasons address the penalty imposed;
- The taxpayer's payment and penalty history;
- The length of time between the event cited as a reason for noncompliance and the subsequent
- compliance; and
- Whether the event that caused the taxpayer's noncompliance could have reasonably been anticipated.

IRM § 20.1.1.3.1.2. Accordingly, the IRS must consider the totality of the circumstances when evaluating a request for penalty abatement. IRM § 20.1.1.3.4(3) ("Each request must be evaluated on its own merit….")

Clearly, the problems with the professionals that the Taxpayers hired directly led to their inability to pay the taxes and the accuracy related errors on the returns. To be saddled with the additional tax penalties would harm the Taxpayers' ability to operate their businesses as well as the Taxpayers' actual ability to pay back taxes due. For these reasons, we respectfully request abatement of all penalties and interest associated with accuracy and failure to pay taxes due for 2013-2016 tax years.

Very truly yours,

TAX PRO NAME

Abatement Request – Medical Issues

February 28, 2020

<u>VIA FAX</u>
SO
Internal Revenue Service
Address Block
Address Block

    Re: TAXPAYER NAME, SSN _____

Dear Sir or Madam:

TAXPAYER had a long history of payment compliance prior to a horrific car accident in 2002, in which the taxpayer suffered lifelong injuries that have impaired her day-to-day life. Moreover, she had a long history of filing compliance until further problems arose in 2012. Due to extensive brain damage as a result of the accident, Ms. TAXPAYER has impaired cognitive ability, which has caused her to lose her job on a nearly annual basis in the highly competitive field she works in. The constant fluctuation in income and change to independent contractor employment status in 2012 has made it nearly impossible for Ms. TAXPAYER to catch up on her tax debt. She has found some stability at her current job, but is required to outlay thousands of dollars of her own money each year to cultivate new client relationships and consistently generate new work.

Ms. TAXPAYER was involved in a serious car accident on October 26, 2002. She was a passenger in a car that sustained major damage to the right side of the car due to a collision with a tree and a light pole. She sustained severe injuries, including internal brain hemorrhage and lacerations to the right arm and leg. Jaws of life were used to extricate Ms. TAXPAYER. We've included photos of the vehicle—it is hard to believe someone could survive such a horrific wreck.

Ever since the accident, Ms. TAXPAYER's life has never been the same. She sustained severe internal brain injuries which majorly impact her day to day life. She has continued word finding difficulty and difficulty thinking. The injury has impaired her short-term memory and cognitive processing.

As the medical reports detail, she suffered from Axonal shearing of the connective tissues in the brain and bleeding. She was unconscious for several days and suffered severely for years having to take speech therapy as well as physical therapy for broken joints in her writing hand and a broken ankle. In 2004-2006, she flunked the Florida bar after four attempts.

Not only has the accident taken a major toll on Ms. TAXPAYER's physical and mental wellbeing—but also her emotional state. She has had bouts of depression, an enhanced startle response, and has less energy. She is also more emotional and quicker to lose her tempter (according to friends and family, Ms. TAXPAYER was previously an easy going person.)

Due to her dramatic change in personality after the accident, her then-husband walked out on her and their three children. She had to prematurely return back to work before fully recuperating, as she was now a single mother. When she returned to work in late November 2002, she was immediately pressured to generate new business. She was criticized by management that she was too emotional. Her boss fired her for "lack of effort" on March 21, 2003. She had been with the firm 19 years. Ever since, she has been unable to hold down a job for a significant period of time.

As Dr. DOCTOR notes in his medical report, "these cognitive and emotional deficits are permanent and have seriously compromised her ability to practice as a lawyer at the level she was able to perform prior to her accident."

In addition to three doctors' reports, we have included a WSJ article on internal brain injuries which describes how patients are known as the "walking wounded" as the injuries are not external but still real and problematic.

As the article discusses, there are numerous issues (including inability to switch mental tracks), and if not for the medicine she takes from the doctor recommended through the National Institute of Health (NIH), she could not stay awake to work through the day and function. While she works very hard and appears normal, she cannot manage new tasks well.

The repeated loss of jobs in 2003, 2006, 2007, 2009, 2011, 2013 took a toll on Ms. TAXPAYER's finances and emotional state. The job she had in 2012 changed her status from an employee with taxes withheld to no withholding and required her to fund extensive national and international travel to try to convince clients to switch firms. She then lost her job again in 2013 and had to start another job in 2014 with no withholding and required her to fund travel to bring in clients. She exhausted all of her pension resources due to job losses and gaps to be rehired and that made catching up with the IRS taxes nearly impossible.

The taxpayer was completely overwhelmed in 2012, starting a job where no taxes were withheld and receiving k-1s in multiple states. Even the CPA she brought them to said he was confused and they were complex and difficult. The taxpayer also lost both of her parents the prior year, after caring for her mother through her battle with liver cancer. It is also important to note that the inheritance she received in 2015 went directly to pay the underpaid taxes from a joint return with her ex-husband that he refused to help pay.

Lastly, Ms. TAXPAYER is also suffering from hypertension and now under medical care from an internist for this medical condition related to the medical damages from the accident. The stress of her tax problems have only worsened the condition.

Ms. TAXPAYER clearly had no intention of disobeying the taxing statutes. It is our contention that requiring Ms. TAXPAYER to pay penalties and interest on those penalties would not support voluntary compliance by taxpayers, as there was clearly no willful intent to disobey the taxing statutes.

Clearly, the medical problems directly led to Ms. TAXPAYER's inability to pay the taxes or file the returns when due. For these reasons, we respectfully requests abatement of all penalties and interest associated with late filing and failure to pay taxes due for 2012-2015 tax years.

Very truly yours,

TAX PRO NAME

Abatement Request – Assorted Issues

February 28, 2020

<u>VIA FEDERAL EXPRESS</u>
Department of the Treasury
Internal Revenue Service
Holtsville, NY 11742-0480

    Re: TAXPAYERS

Dear Sir or Madam:

This office represents the above-referenced taxpayers, HUSBAND ("Mr. TAXPAYER") and WIFE ("Mrs. TAXPAYER" or collectively with Mr. TAXPAYER, "Taxpayers") before the Internal Revenue Service (the "IRS"). The IRS has assessed failure to file and failure to pay penalties against the Taxpayer for tax years 2017, 2018 and 2019. For the following reasons, we request that the IRS abate all penalties for tax years 2017 through and including 2019, as well as any corresponding interest from those penalties.

The Taxpayers have had a long history of complying with their federal tax obligations and have never been significantly penalized prior to tax years 2017-2019. There were a series of compelling and devastating events that directly led to their tax issues. The Taxpayers have made every effort to resolve their tax issues since the period at issue. They have (1) attempted to obtain first-time penalty abatement on tax year 2017 but were denied because there was a computer-generated penalty abatement for tax year 2014 for $1.63 (this de minimis amount has prevented the taxpayers from abatement relief in 2017) and (2) set up an installment agreement to full pay their IRS debt.

Background

Mr. TAXPAYER is the eldest of his siblings—the care of his immediate family has always fallen on his shoulders. In August of 2016, his mother was diagnosed with cancer. She was in treatment for a year (until the end of 2017). During this time, Mr. TAXPAYER spent significant time aiding in her recovery.

In September 2016, Mr. TAXPAYER's grandfather (his mother's father) suffered a stroke, was hospitalized and then admitted to a nursing home for a year until his passing on August 13, 2017. Mr. TAXPAYER was constantly by his side and tending to his care, as well as consoling his mother (who was still recovering from her own health issues).

In January 2017, Mrs. TAXPAYER gave birth to the Taxpayers' tenth child. Their eldest child was 17 at the time. Having an infant in addition to tending to the needs of nine other children was overwhelming and financially difficult.

In November 2017, Mrs. TAXPAYER's mother slipped and fell on ice—her injuries left her immobile for over a year. She underwent surgery and physical therapy during this time. Mrs. TAXPAYER, who lived in close proximity to her mother, was the one taking care of her.

Also in November of 2017, Mr. TAXPAYER's sister gave birth to a micro-preemie at 23 weeks; the baby had a very low chance of survival. Mr. TAXPAYER was the one who was there for his family at all times, giving physical and emotional support.

In January 2019, Mrs. TAXPAYER suffered a major gall stone attack, with many attacks to follow for about a year. Three of these attacks required hospitalization. It was very difficult for the family to care for their ten children, including a toddler, while Mrs. TAXPAYER was unwell.

In June of 2019, Mr. TAXPAYER's mother was diagnosed with Guillain-Barré syndrome (GBS). She was partially paralyzed for six months and completely relied on the care and support of Mr. TAXPAYER.

Penalty Abatement

In sum, from the end of 2016 until the end of 2019, it was a very tumultuous and traumatic time for the Taxpayers. While the aforementioned events were transpiring, the Taxpayers were also taking care of the needs of their family of 12. Not only was their attention diverted from focusing on their taxes, but they were unexpectedly spending money that was earmarked for taxes to help support troubled family members.

Given the myriad issues surrounding the Taxpayers from 2016-2019, the Taxpayers have reasonable cause for abatement of penalties. The Taxpayers clearly had no intention of disobeying tax laws. Requiring them to pay penalties and interest on those penalties would not support voluntary compliance by Taxpayers, as there was clearly no willful intent to disobey the taxing statutes.

These issues directly led to Mr. and Mrs. TAXPAYER's inability to pay the taxes or file the returns when due. The Taxpayers have worked tirelessly to ensure these delays do not occur again and have worked with the Service to resolve the outstanding liabilities. For these reasons, we respectfully request abatement of all penalties and interest associated with late filing and failure to pay taxes due for the 2017, 2018 and 2019 tax years.

Please call with any questions or if any additional information is required.

Very truly yours,

TAX PRO NAME

Abatement Request – Dementia

February 28, 2020

<u>VIA FEDERAL EXPRESS</u>
Internal Revenue Service
Service Center Penalty Appeals Coordinator
P.O. Box 9941 TPR M/S 6731
Ogden, UT 84409

    Re: TAXPAYER'S FATHER

Dear Sir or Madam:

I am writing regarding the above referenced taxpayer to respectfully request penalty abatement for tax periods 3/2017, 12/2017, 6/2018, 9/2018, 12/2018, 3/2019, 6/2019, and 9/2019.

The above referenced taxpayer suffered from Alzheimer's disease and Dementia which was diagnosed in December 2011. In 2013 the taxpayer required 24/7 home care and hired caregivers as household employees. As the taxpayer's health started deteriorating, he had a friend handle payroll for the household employees through Paychex. The taxpayer died 5 months ago. Copies of his medical diagnosis and his death certificate are attached, as is a copy of our IRS Form 2848.

The taxpayer's son then received correspondence from Paychex that made him realize Paychex had not filed quarterly 941s or the annual 940 return. Once it was brought to his attention that Paychex was not filing or paying quarterly and annual payroll tax returns and taxes, the son immediately filed missing returns and mailed payments for tax assessments.

Prior to this disease the taxpayer always maintained a good history of compliance and had no intentions on disobeying the taxing statutes. For these reasons I am respectfully requesting abatement of all penalties and interest associated with late filing and failure to pay taxes due for 2017-2019.

Very truly yours,

TAX PRO NAME

Abatement Request – Form 5500 Penalty

February 28, 2020

<u>VIA FEDERAL EXPRESS</u>
Department of the Treasury
Internal Revenue Service
Ogden, UT 84201

  Re: **TAXPAYER'S FATHER**

Dear Sir or Madam:

Please accept this letter in furtherance of the taxpayer, PLAN NAME ("Taxpayer" or "TAXPAYER'S PLAN"), request for penalty abatement on tax year 2018.

The Taxpayer has had a long history of compliance prior to issues that arose with his accountant and his personal life, which caused the instant issue. The Taxpayer's accountant, ACCOUNTANT ("MR. ACCOUNTANT") of ACCOUNTING FIRM ("ACCOUNTING FIRM"), provided services for the Taxpayer since the early 1990s. According to New York State Division of Corporations, ACCOUNTING FIRM was established on December 9, 1992. The Taxpayer became a client shortly thereafter.

TAXPAYER, the owner of the TAXPAYER'S PLAN entrusted ACCOUTING FIRM to provide accounting services and prepare and file his individual tax returns in addition to the preparation and filing of the Form 5500 for the Plan.

TAXPAYER is a self-employed physician, who, in addition to his medical responsibilities, manages the business of his practice. Due to his demanding career and lifestyle, he delegated his tax matters to qualified professionals. In order to ensure the TAXPAYER'S PLAN Form 5500 is prepared, TAXPAYER has duplicate copies of the TAXPAYER'S PLAN monthly brokerage statements sent directly to ACCOUNTANT (see Exhibit A). Because duplicate copies of the statements are sent directly to ACCOUNTANT by the brokerage house, TAXPAYER feels secure ACCOUNTANT has timely receipt of pertinent information necessary to complete Form 5500.
ACCOUNTANT timely filed Form 5558 Application for Extension so the taxpayer had no

reason to believe the return would not be prepared and filed upon its due date (see Exhibit B).

At the time of the due date of his 2018 Form 5500, TAXPAYER life was especially chaotic. TAXPAYER is the sole caregiver for his elderly widowed mother. In fall 2019, her dementia was quickly progressing. There was no one else in the family who could help–he has one sibling in Florida and one in California. All of his mother's care lies on his shoulders. Accordingly, his attention was diverted to caring for his mother's deteriorating health.

Further to the issues in TAXPAYER personal life, he has always faithfully relied on his accountant. ACCOUNTANT has a long history of managing TAXPAYER tax obligations in an efficient and careful way. By way of example, ACCOUNTANT timely filed Form 5558; it was sent it via certified mail and tracking information was retained. ACCOUNTANT admits that it appears the 2018 Form 5500 was never prepared; it was inadvertently missed in the very hectic October 15, 2019 filing deadline. TAXPAYER Form 5500s were timely filed for Plan Numbers 001 and 002 (see Exhibit C); he was mistakenly unaware that Number 003 was not prepared or filed. ACCOUNTANT has accepted fault for the missed filing.

Once ACCOUNTANT discovered that he mistakenly did not file the 2018 Form 5500 (while he was preparing the 2019 filing in October 2020), he sprang into action. He immediately filed the return and included a letter requesting abatement of the penalties. Unfortunately, it is unclear if the IRS did not review the request or simply denied it. However, due to the CP283's issuance, it appears the Taxpayer no longer qualifies under the IRS' delinquent filer program under Revenue Procedure 2015-32.

The Taxpayer timely filed the 2019 Form 5500, as he has done every year but for tax year 2018. The Taxpayer clearly had no intention of disobeying the taxing statutes. Penalties for late filing the Form 5500 are governed by IRC §§ 6652 and 6692. In section 6652, it states a taxpayer can have the penalties abated if it can establish that the failure to comply with the rules was due to reasonable cause.

Neither ACCOUNTANT nor TAXPAYER were familiar with the permanent program for Delinquent Filer Penalty Relief (Rev. Proc. 2015-32) and did not file a Form 14704,

Transmittal Schedule when the 2018 Form 5500 was late filed. Given that the oversight of the unfiled return was discovered amidst a pandemic and the taxpayer had not heard of the program (which has changed form over the years and is somewhat obscure), the taxpayer respectfully requests either 1) abatement under reasonable cause or 2) entry into the program.

Please call me should you have any questions.

Very truly yours,

TAX PRO NAME

Abatement Request – Payroll Company Theft

October 8, 2020

<u>Via Fax: xxx-xx-xxxx</u>
Internal Revenue Service
Attn: Revenue Officer
Address

RE: Taxpayer

Dear Revenue Officer,

This office is counsel to the above-referenced taxpayers, Business Name.

This taxpayer hired a payroll company, Payroll Business Name, to handle its payroll. The taxpayer had funds withdrawn from their payroll account at Big Bank on a regular basis by Payroll Business Name payroll for the payment of their Federal Tax Deposits. However, it appears from the IRS transcripts received from Revenue Officer that these funds were not advanced to the IRS. The payroll company was fully responsible for the timely filings of returns and payment of payroll taxes. In all years since they began business, the payroll company had filed all the returns and advanced all the monies in a timely manner. The taxpayer had no reason to question their activities as the funds were being withdrawn from their bank account on a regular basis. When the company became aware that money it had paid did not reach the IRS it terminated its relationship with Payroll Business Name immediately. They then made sure all missing tax payments were made immediately for any missing quarter in conjunction with all filings submitted by their accountant.

Attached we have provided copies of the taxpayer's payroll account bank statements showing the timely withdrawals of funds, copies of the payroll history reports and the taxpayers spreadsheets which show the amount owed to the government in payroll taxes. We request that the penalties incurred by the taxpayer for tax periods ended 3/31/2018, 6/30/2018, 9/30 2018, 12/31/2018, 3/31/2019, 6/30/2019, 9/30/2019 and 12/31/2019 for any late payments of taxes, late filing and not making their FTD's timely be abated as they did everything in their power to comply with their payroll requirements and it is solely because of the actions of the outside payroll company that their funds were not remitted to the IRS when the payroll company had them.

If you have any questions, please contact me at (XXX) XXX-XXXX.

Thank you,

Tax Rep

Refund Claims

Cover Letter – Form 843

June 9, 2017

<u>VIA Certified Mail</u>
Department of the Treasury
Internal Revenue Service
P.O. Box 9019
Holtsville, NY 11742-9019

    Re: **Taxpayer Name, SSN xxx-xx-xxxx**
           Form 843, Claim for Refund and Request for Abatement

Dear Sir or Madam:

Enclosed please find the following documents:

1. Form 843 Claim for Refund and Request for Abatement for tax year 2015; and
2. Letter of Explanation with attached exhibits and medical documentation.

Very truly yours,

TAX PRO NAME

Appeal for Refund – Past 3 Years

June 9, 2017

<u>VIA Overnight Mail</u>
Department of the Treasury
Internal Revenue Service
Office of Appeals
P.O. Box 9054
Andover, MA 01810-9054

   Re: **Taxpayer Name, SSN xxx-xx-xxxx**
      Appeal of Refund Denial for Tax Year 2011 Pursuant to IRC §6511(h)

Dear Sir or Madam:

This office represents the taxpayer, TAXPAYER ("Taxpayer" or "Ms. TAXPAYER"), before the Internal Revenue Service (the "IRS"). We are in receipt of your letter dated June 23, 2017 (the "Denial Letter") denying the Taxpayer a refund in the amount of $11,774.00 for tax year ending December 31, 2011. The Denial Letter is attached hereto as **Exhibit A**. For the following reasons, we request that the IRS allow the Taxpayer a full refund in the amount of $11,774.00 for tax year 2011.

The Taxpayer is seeking the $11,774.00 refund from 2011, despite having filed her original tax return for 2011 more than three years after the due date, pursuant to 26 U.S.C. § 6511(h). 26 U.S.C. §6511(h) provides in relevant part that the running of the period of limitation is suspended during any period of an individual's life when that individual is financially disabled. 26 U.S.C. § 6511(h)(2) defines a financially disabled individual as one who is "unable to manage his financial affairs by reason of a medically determinable physical or mental impairment of the individual which can be expected to result in death or which has lasted or can be expected to last for a continuous period of not less than 12 months." Internal Revenue Manual 25.6.1.10.2.9.1 (05-17-2004) provides that financial disability can be shown through a written statement from a medical physician stating a medical opinion that the impairment prevented the taxpayer from managing his or her financial affairs during the period in question.

Ms. TAXPAYER had a long history of compliance with her tax obligations with her late husband, HUSBAND. This good history was disrupted after a culmination of events, including the death of HUSBAND and her best friend, FRIEND, within a short period of time. These circumstances would have been disruptive for anyone, but Ms. TAXPAYER suffers from several psychiatric conditions, including depression, post-traumatic stress disorder and borderline personality disorder, and these circumstances left her in a major depressive episode, unable to handle many aspects of her life, including her finances. Ms. TAXPAYER's psychiatric conditions are further detailed in letters from her treating psychiatrists, DOC 1, M.D. and DOC 2, M.D., which are attached hereto as **Exhibit B** and **Exhibit C**, respectively.

As **Exhibit B** and **Exhibit C** illustrate, due to a childhood filled with abuse Ms. TAXPAYER has always struggled with organization and getting paperwork done. Throughout their marriage, Robert handled all the household bills and taxes. After Robert's death, Ms. TAXPAYER found herself in a state of paralysis and a major depressive episode with suicidal thoughts. In the years since HUSBAND's death Ms. TAXPAYER had no choice but to focus her all of her attention on her mental health and well-being. She has undergone significant therapy and hospitalization at the psychiatric inpatient ward, and has worked with her psychiatrist to tailor medications to best meet her needs. Once stabilized Ms. TAXPAYER decided it was time to shift her focus to an issue that had taken the backseat, her finances. With the help and support of her children Ms. TAXPAYER filed her tax returns for tax years 2011 through 2015 in early 2017.

Based on the letters from Ms. TAXPAYER's treating psychiatrists it is clear that the period of limitations was suspended for more than 12 consecutive months pursuant to 26 U.C.C. § 6511(h) while Ms. TAXPAYER was suffering from a major depressive episode with suicidal ideations. Both DOC 1 and DOC 2 provided a medical opinion that Ms. TAXPAYER's physical and mental impairments prevented her from managing her financial affairs. As stated in both letters, "Is it likely that her Post Traumatic Stress Disorder, her depression, her borderline personality disorder, her husband's and her closest friends' deaths contributed to Ms. TAXPAYER's inability to get things done in her life in an organized way during these past several years? The answer is yes..... All of these symptoms likely contributed to her failure to deal with issues like the payment of taxes in a timely way."

Based on the facts presented of Ms. TAXPAYER's financial disability, including the medical opinion of two of her treating psychiatrists, we are asking the IRS to allow Ms. TAXPAYER the $11,774.00 refund for tax year 2011. Additionally, a copy of Form 2848, Power of Attorney is attached hereto. Please contact me after you have reviewed this package.

Under penalty of perjury, I declare that I prepared the written statement and accompanying documents. To the best of my knowledge the protest and accompanying documents are true and correct.

Very truly yours,

TAX PRO NAME

Summons Response

Letter to Potential Client About IRS Summons

March ___, 20___

Potential Client's Name
Street Address
City, State Zip

Re: IRS Summons

Dear POTENTIAL TAXPAYER:

You explained to us that you had received an IRS administrative summons and wanted more information about what it meant.

An Administrative Summons is an order issued by the Internal Revenue Service to a person or entity, requiring them to provide information or documents related to their tax payments or finances. It is an important tool utilized by the IRS in determining whether individuals and businesses are complying with federal tax laws.

Typically, an administrative summons will be issued when the IRS believes that someone has failed to comply with tax laws or has not provided the necessary information needed for an audit. When a summons is issued, it must be served on the individual or entity being investigated either personally, through mail, or through third-party delivery services. Upon receipt of the summons, the summoned party must then respond within a certain timeframe either providing all requested information and documents or, if personally summoned, to appear in the designated IRS office.

If you fail to comply with a summons the IRS will send your case to the IRS Office of Chief Counsel who will send a letter admonishing you for not showing up and providing you with a new date. Failure to comply with the new date will result in your case being referred to the United States Attorney's office and can result in either hefty fines, criminal prosecution or both.

Once a response has been received from the summoned party and verified as accurate, the IRS will then look at this information and other evidence gathered as part of its investigation into any potential tax violations. The agency may then make adjustments or pursue further legal remedies as deemed appropriate in each specific case. This could include making changes to past returns, issuing refunds for overpayment of taxes, seeking payment for unpaid taxes due to discrepancies in reporting income, levying assets such as bank accounts held by taxpayers etc.

The IRS administrative summons process can be complicated and intimidating for those unfamiliar with how it works but understanding it is essential if you want to ensure compliance and protect yourself from severe punishments imposed by law. If you receive an IRS summons, always seek professional advice before making any decisions about responding or taking action against it.

We are here if you want help with this matter. Just contact us at (xxx) xxx-xxxx or email at EMAIL ADDRESS and we can get you in for a consult and see what needs to be done.

Sincerely,

Tax Rep's Name

Letter to Revenue Officer About IRS Summons

March ___, 20___

Internal Revenue Service
Att: _____, Revenue Officer
Street Address
City, State Zip

Re: Administrative Summons

Dear REVENUE OFFICER'S NAME:

We received the administrative summons you issued for the taxpayer's records for the tax years _____.

We are preparing the returns and expect to have them signed and delivered to you by _____, 20___. Therefore, we wanted to let you know we did not plan to come to your office on the date you indicated on the Summons, but also that we are not ignoring it but know you need the returns, and we think it best to just prepare and deliver them to you.

Please contact me and confirm this is acceptable. I can be reached at (xxx) xxx-xxxx or by email at EMAIL ADDRESS. Thank you.

Sincerely,

Tax Rep's Name

Tax Levies

Letter to General Contractor – Levy on Subcontractor

June 9, 2017

<u>Business Name</u>
Business Address
City, State and Zip

    Re: **Subcontractor IRS Notice of Levy**

Dear GENERAL CONTRACTOR:

We are tax counsel representing SUBCONTRACTOR in his matter with the Internal Revenue Service.

I have reviewed the Form 668-A Notice of Levy, dated _____, and am writing to inform you that this Levy is not a Continuing Levy, and therefore applies only moneys earned by SUBCONTRACTOR and owed to him as of the date you received the levy from the IRS.

If there were no funds due Mr. SUBCONTRACTOR as of that date, then you do not have to send any money to the IRS and it can be ignored.

If you have any questions regarding this matter, please feel free to contact me directly at (203) XXX-XXXX.

Very truly yours,

TAX PRO NAME

Fax to RO – Request Partial Release of Levy

One Audubon Street, 3rd Floor
New Haven, CT 06511
(203) 285-8545
(203) 286-1311
www.gs-lawfirm.com

Fax

To:	REVENUE OFFICER NAME	**From:**	Eric L. Green
Fax:	(855) xxx-xxxx	**Pages:**	1
Phone:	(203) XXX-XXXX	**Date:**	December 3, 2020
Re:	Taxpayer Name	**cc:**	

Comments:

REVENUE OFFICER NAME,

We received copies of the notice of levy which took $5,100 from the client's bank account. As we discussed on the phone, I understand your reluctance to release the levy, however the taxpayer will be unable to pay their rent or health insurance without some of the levied funds being released.

Attached are copies of his rent, his health insurance, and copies of the checks written that will now bounce. If you agree, please release back to the taxpayer the $2,830 he needs to pay both of these amounts.

Thank you, and if you wish to discuss this further, please call me immediately as time is of the essence with this issue.

TAX PRO NAME

Fax to RO – Request Release of Levy of Payroll Account

One Audubon Street, 3rd Floor
New Haven, CT 06511
(203) 285-8545
(203) 286-1311
www.gs-lawfirm.com

Fax

To:	REVENUE OFFICER NAME	**From:**	Eric L. Green
Fax:	(855) xxx-xxxx	**Pages:**	1
Phone:	(203) XXX-XXXX	**Date:**	December 3, 2020
Re:	Taxpayer Name	**cc:**	

Comments:

REVENUE OFFICER NAME,

We received copies of the notice of levy. I have expressed to the taxpayer the urgency to get the documents you requested.

I am asking that you release the levy on account xxxxx-3476. I have attached a screen shot of this and please note the account is their payroll account. You should also note that Paychex just attempted to pull the payroll and it failed (see the entry with yesterday's date for $8,342). This money obviously does not belong to the Taxpayer but rather must be paid into the IRS and State of Connecticut. If you could please fax us over the release, we will fax you back the proof of the tax payments so you can see that the money did in fact get taken by Paychex for the taxes.

Thank you,

TAX PRO NAME

Letter for Release of Levy Due to Hardship

<u>FEDEX</u>

January ___, 20____

Revenue Officer A. Smith
Internal Revenue Service
Street Address
City, State Zip

Re: Levy on TAXPAYER'S NAME, SSN ****

Dear Ms. Smith,

We submitted the 433-A you requested along with all of the taxpayer's supporting documentation. As we discussed you agree with our conclusion that the Taxpayer has no ability to pay and should have their account placed in "Uncollectible" status. Despite this, however, you indicated that you had no intention of releasing the levy on the taxpayer's wages because of the taxpayer's missing 2019 return.

I wanted to point out that you are legally obligated to release the levy regardless of the taxpayer's compliance. Pursuant to IRC § 6343 a levy must be released if it is causing economic hardship, which is defined as someone who is "Uncollectible." The United States Tax Court has reiterated this in its decision in *Kathleen A. Vinatieri v. Commissioner, Docket No. 15895-08L (2009)*.

In its decision, the United States Court stated:

> Under regulations prescribed by the Secretary, the Secretary must release a levy upon all, or part of, a taxpayer's property or rights to property if, inter alia, the Secretary has determined that the levy is creating an economic hardship due to the financial condition of the taxpayer. Sec. 6343(a)(1)(D), I.R.C. The regulations provide that a levy is creating an economic hardship due to the financial condition of an individual taxpayer and must be released "if satisfaction of the levy in whole or in part will cause an individual taxpayer to be unable to pay his or her reasonable basic living expenses." Sec. 301.6343-1(b)(4), Proced. & Admin. Regs.

Sec. 6343(a)(1)(D), I.R.C., and sec. 301.6343-1(b)(4), Proced. & Admin. Regs., require release of a levy that creates an economic hardship regardless of the taxpayer's noncompliance with filing required returns.

If you disagree, please respond in writing explaining your authority. Otherwise please release the levy and fax us a copy of the release. I will continue to work with the taxpayer to get the missing return completed and filed with you.

I can be reached at (xxx) xxx-xxxx if you wish to discuss this further.

Very truly yours,

YOUR NAME

Tax Liens

Tax Lien Documents Checklist

- Copy of the Deed to the Property
- Sales Contract
- Title Search
- Appraisal by the Bank
- Payoff's From Liens Ahead of the IRS
- Proposed Settlement Statement

Letter for Discharge – Both Spouses Liable

June 9, 2017

<u>Fax: 855-390-3530</u>
Centralized Lien Operation
P.O. Box 145595
Stop 8420G
Cincinnati, OH 45250-5595

    Re: **Discharge of RESIDENCE from the Federal Tax Lien**

Dear Sir or Madam:

Enclosed please find the TAXPAYERs Application for Certificate of Discharge for discharging their home, located at _____ MAIN STREET, CITY, STATE ZIP from the federal Tax Lien, including:

1. A copy of our Power of Attorney, Form 2848
2. The Form 14135, Application for Certificate of Discharge
3. Copy of the Deed to the Property
5. Sales Contract
6. Title Search
7. Appraisal by the Bank
8. Payoff's From Liens Ahead of the IRS
9. Proposed Settlement Statement
10. Copy of the estimated cost to move the family to their new rental

The Taxpayers owes the IRS approximately $220,000. He and his wife are selling their home to a third party and the sale is expected to provide them $180,000. The taxpayer's are requesting a Discharge of the house from the tax lien in exchange for the $180,000 of sale proceeds.

If you have any questions regarding this application, please contact me directly at (203) xxx-xxxx.

Very truly yours,

TAX PRO NAME

C. Taxpayers

Letter for Discharge – Only One Spouse Liable

June 9, 2017

Fax: 855-390-3530
Centralized Lien Operation
P.O. Box 145595
Stop 8420G
Cincinnati, OH 45250-5595

Re: Discharge of RESIDENCE from the Federal Tax Lien

Dear Sir or Madam:

Enclosed please find the TAXPAYER's Application for Certificate of Discharge for discharging their home, located at _____ MAIN STREET, CITY, STATE ZIP from the federal Tax Lien, including:

1. A copy of our Power of Attorney, Form 2848
2. The Form 14135, Application for Certificate of Discharge
3. Copy of the Deed to the Property
4. Sales Contract
5. Title Search
6. Appraisal by the Bank
7. Payoff's From Liens Ahead of the IRS
8. Proposed Settlement Statement

The Taxpayer owes the IRS approximately $220,000. He and his wife, who is not liable for the tax debt, are selling their home to a third party and the sale is expected to provide them $180,000. The Taxpayer's portion of that (50%, or about $90,000) would be paid to the IRS in exchange for it discharging the home from the tax Lien.

If you have any questions regarding this application, please contact me directly at (203) xxx-xxxx.

Very truly yours,

TAX PRO NAME

C. Taxpayers

Letter for Discharge – Carve Out Moving Costs

June 9, 2017

<u>Fax: 855-390-3530</u>
Centralized Lien Operation
P.O. Box 145595
Stop 8420G
Cincinnati, OH 45250-5595

Re: Discharge of RESIDENCE from the Federal Tax Lien

Dear Sir or Madam:

Enclosed please find the TAXPAYERs Application for Certificate of Discharge for discharging their home, located at _____ MAIN STREET, CITY, STATE ZIP from the federal Tax Lien, including:

1. A copy of our Power of Attorney, Form 2848
2. The Form 14135, Application for Certificate of Discharge
3. Copy of the Deed to the Property
4. Sales Contract
5. Title Search
6. Appraisal by the Bank
7. Payoff's From Liens Ahead of the IRS
8. Proposed Settlement Statement
9. Copy of the estimated cost to move the family to their new rental

The Taxpayers owes the IRS approximately $220,000. He and his wife are selling their home to a third party and the sale is expected to provide them $180,000. The taxpayer's are requesting a Discharge of the house from the tax lien in exchange for $170,000 of the proceeds. The other $10,000 is necessary for them to cover the cost of vacating their home and to move their family to a place they will be renting. We have enclosed the estimate from MOVING COMPANY.

If you have any questions regarding this application, please contact me directly at (203) xxx-xxxx.

Very truly yours,

TAX PRO NAME

C. Taxpayers

Letter for Lien Subordination

June 9, 2017

<u>Fax: 844-201-8382</u>
Advisory Consolidated Receipts
7940 Kentucky Drive
Stop 2850F
Florence, KY 41042

Re: Request for Certificate of Subordination

Dear Sir or Madam:

Enclosed please find the TAXPAYERs Application for a Certificate of Subordination of the federal tax lien so they may refinance their current mortgage. The refinance will enable the Taxpayers to reduce their monthly mortgage and therefore increase their monthly installment payments to the IRS by $320.

Enclosed are the following documents:

1. A copy of our Power of Attorney, Form 2848
2. The Form 14134, Application for Certificate of Subordination
3. Copy of the Deed to the Property
4. New Mortgage Commitment by the Bank
5. Title Search
6. Appraisal by the Bank
7. Payoff's From Liens Ahead of the IRS
8. Proposed Settlement Statement

If you have any questions regarding this application, please contact me directly at (203) xxx-xxxx.

Very truly yours,

TAX PRO NAME

C. Taxpayers

Letter for Lien Withdrawal

June 9, 2017

<u>Fax: 844-201-8382</u>
Advisory Consolidated Receipts
7940 Kentucky Drive
Stop 2850F
Florence, KY 41042

    Re: **Request for Lien Withdrawal**

Dear Sir or Madam:

Enclosed please find the TAXPAYER's form 12277, Application for Withdrawal of the Notice of Federal Tax Lien.

The Taxpayer has made three direct-debit installment payments pursuant to his installment agreement and his balance is now below $25,000. Per IRM Section 5.12.9.3.2.1, the Taxpayer meets the special provisions for withdrawal under a direct debit installment agreement.

If you have any questions regarding this application, please contact me directly at (203) xxx-xxxx.

Very truly yours,

TAX PRO NAME

C. Taxpayers

Letter to Town Clerk – With Lien Release and Payment

August 9, 2019

<u>VIA CERTIFIED MAIL</u>
CITY Town Clerk
Address
City, State & Zip

    Re: **TAXPAYER**

        Address

Dear Town Clerk,

The following document is enclosed for filing on the Connecticut land records:

Certificate of Discharge of Property From Federal Tax Lien

A check in the amount of $60.00 is enclosed for your required fee.

Very truly yours,

TAX PRO NAME

Letter Applying for Certificate of Non-Attachment

June 9, 2017

<u>Fax: 844-201-8382</u>
Advisory Consolidated Receipts
7940 Kentucky Drive
Stop 2850F
Florence, KY 41042

    Re: **Certificate of Non-Attachment for 1000 Main Street, New Haven, CT**

Dear Sir or Madam,

This is my application for a Certificate of Non-Attachment.

1. Name: TAXPAYER'S SPOUSE
2. The Certificate of Non-Attachment is necessary because I am attempting to refinance my home and my wife, who owes money to the IRS has a lien against her. Though she has never had any ownership interest in the property described in #3 below, the bank is refusing to refinance my mortgage without the Certificate of Non-Attachment.
3. The property is the single-family home located at 1000 Main Street, New Haven, Connecticut. Attached to this as exhibits are a copy of the deed to the property.
4. Attached are the copies of the federal Tax Liens I obtained from the land records. I believe this is all of them.
    - They were filed against WIFE'S NAME and she resides at 1000 Main Street, New Haven, CT;
    - The Notice of Federal Tax Liens wee filed on _{DATE}_____ and on ___{DATE}_____
    - The serial number shown on the notices of lien are _____ and _____.
5. WIFE, whom the liens are filed against, has never had any interest in the property located at 1000 Main Street, New Haven, CT.
6. WIFE's NAME is my legal spouse.

7. At the time the Notices of Federal Tax Lien were filed I also resided at 1000 Main Street, New Haven, Connecticut
8. My social security number is _____.
9. My daytime telephone number is _____.
10. My representative is TAX PRO NAME and their address is _____

"Under penalties of perjury, I declare that I have examined this application, including any accompanying schedules, exhibits, affidavits, and statements, and to the best of my knowledge and belief, it is true, correct, and complete.

_____   _____
Name   Date

Uncollectible Status

IRS Collection Document Checklist - Individual

{Please provide us all that apply}

General:

- Have you filed all your federal tax returns? Yes ☐ No ☐
    - If No, which years remain unfiled?
    - Are the tax returns prepared?
- Have you filed all of your state tax returns? Yes ☐ No ☐
    - If No, which states do you need to file in?
    - What tax years remain to be filed?
    - Are the tax returns prepared?
- Has either the IRS or state taxing authority contacted you? Yes ☐ No ☐
    - If Yes, please provide copies of any correspondence you have received

Assets:

- Do you have a bank account? Yes ☐ No ☐ • If Yes, please provide copies of the bank statements for the last six months of bank statements for all accounts
- Do you own any investments (stocks, bonds, mutual funds, etc.) Yes ☐ No ☐ • Most recent statement for all investment accounts (Stocks, Mutual Funds, Trading Accounts)
- Do you have any retirement accounts (IRA, 401(k), 403(b), etc.)? Yes ☐ No ☐ • Copies of all 401(k) and 403(b) plan documents
    - Statements of value for all other investments, including documentation of loans against any investment
- Do you own any virtual currency, or have you owned any virtual currency in the last 6 years? Yes ☐ No ☐
    - Statement of value of anything you currently own
    - If you previously owned virtual currency and sold it please confirm it was reported on your tax returns that were filed with the IRS. Yes ☐ No ☐
- Do you own or have you owned any foreign assets, trusts, or bank accounts in the last 6 years? Yes ☐ No ☐
    - List any foreign assets currently owned

- o If it includes foreign bank or investment accounts, please provide the last 6 months of statements on all foreign accounts
- o If you sold or transferred the assets, please confirm you reported the assets/transactions on your tax returns? Yes ☐ No ☐
- Life Insurance • Statement showing the premium and cash value of life insurance
- Do you own any real estate? Yes ☐ No ☐ If No go to #8 • Printouts for the value of any real estate owned (appraisal, Zillow, etc.)
    - o Recent mortgage statements for any property owned
    - o Recent statement for credit lines/home equity loans secured by any real estate
- Do you rent your home? Yes ☐ No ☐
    - o Lease agreement
    - o Utility bills
    - o Proof of rental payments for the last 6 months
- Do you own 1 or more automobiles? Yes ☐ No ☐ • Kelly Blue Book printouts for value of each vehicle
    - o Recent monthly statement of any loan balance and monthly payment
    - o Recent monthly statement showing the lease payment and time remaining on the lease
- Do you own any collectables (artwork, jewelry, collections, etc.)? Yes ☐ No ☐ • Statement of value or appraisal for collectables
    - o Copy of your homeowners or renter's insurance including riders.

Income & Expenses:

- We need your current income for you and your spouse/partner/significant other you reside with/anyone who contributes to the household income (whether they are responsible or not). Please get us any of the following if they apply:
    - o A current profit and loss for each business or rental activity
    - o If you or your spouse are wage earners, your three most recent pay stubs
    - o Proof of any social security income
    - o Proof of annuity or retirement income
    - o Proof of any child support or alimony received
    - o Proof of any other income or cash flow stream into the household
- Last three months of utility bills

- Proof of your mortgage payment and balance. If you rent, we need your current lease agreement
- Proof of monthly car payments, whether loan or lease, with the balance remaining
- Proof of health insurance and premium amount
- Proof of life insurance premiums
- Proof of disability insurance premiums
- Proof of any alimony or child support you or your spouse pay, including the divorce or separation agreement and court order
- Home equity statement
- Proof of any judgments and payment plans to secured creditors
- Proof of any payment plans with state taxing authorities
- Proof of student loan balances and payments
- Proof of current estimated tax payments (unless you are a wage earner, in which case they are reflected on your paystubs)
- Proof of out-of-pocket healthcare expenses, IF they exceed $52/per person per month (or $114/month for anyone 65 or older)
- Proof of child/dependent care expense, such as daycare and after-school programs
- Proof of any other necessary expenses, such as mandatory union dues, restitution payments, etc.

IRS Collection Document Checklist - Business

{Please provide us all that apply for EACH business owned}

General:

- Has the business filed all federal tax returns? Yes ☐ No ☐
    - If No, which years remain unfiled?
    - Are the tax returns prepared?
- Has the business filed all of its state tax returns? Yes ☐ No ☐
    - If No, which states do you need to file in?
    - What tax years remain to be filed?
    - Are the tax returns prepared?
- Has either the IRS or state taxing authority contacted the business? Yes ☐ No ☐
    - If Yes, please provide copies of any correspondence you have received

Business Information:

Entity Information

- Name_____
- Address:_____
___
- Federal ID Number_____
- Entity Type (Circle One): Sole Prop / LLC / Partnership / C Corp / S Corp / Trust / Estate
- Does the business have employees?   Yes / No
- If Yes please provide us with copies of the payroll information (number of employees, payroll tax returns and if the company is enrolled in EFTPS)
- Does the business utilize a payment processor, like Paypal, Google, etc include virtual currency)   Yes / No
    - If Yes, list them
    _____
- Does the business accept Credit Cards?   Yes / No
    - If Yes, provide us the list of cards accepted by the business
- Provide us with the names, addresses and ownership percentage of all the owners and officers of the business

- Does the business utilize a payroll processor? Yes / No
- Is the business a party to a lawsuit? Yes / No
- Has the business ever filed bankruptcy? Yes / No
- Do any related parties owe money to the business? Yes / No
- Have any assets been transferred from the business within the last 10 years for less than fair market value? Yes / No
- Do you anticipate an increase or decrease in income? Yes / No
    - If "Yes" explain why

Assets:

- Cash: please provide the last 6 months of statements for all bank accounts
- Receivables: provide a list of all the amounts owed to the business, by whom, how much and how old the receivable is
- Lines of Credit: Provide statements for all lines of credit
- Real Property: Provide a list of any real property owned, its Fair-Market Value, and provide statements showing the amounts owed and monthly mortgage balances.
- Vehicles: List all of the vehicles owned by the business, including the year, make, model and mileage on the vehicles. Also provide statements for any loans outstanding on the vehicles
- Furniture and Equipment: Provide a listing of all the business equipment owned by the business and any loans against it. If possible, please provide a depreciation schedule if you have one.
- Business Debts: Please provide statements showing any balances due and monthly payment amounts.

Income & Expenses:

- Please provide all of the following reports:
    - A profit and loss year-to-date
    - The tax returns for the last three years (or as many years as you have)
    - A current cash-flow statement, if you have one

Uncollectible Status Document Checklist

{Please provide us all that apply}

Tax Returns:

- Last three years of tax returns

IRS Notices:

- Copies of any IRS notices, especially if received via certified mail

Assets:

- Bank Accounts
    - Last six months of bank statements for all accounts
- Investments
    - Most recent statement for all investment accounts (Stocks, Mutual Funds, Trading Accounts)
    - Most recent statement for all retirement accounts (IRA, 401(k), 403(b), etc)
    - Copies of all 401(k) and 403(b) plan documents
    - Statements of value for all other investments, including documentation of loans against any investment
- Virtual Currency (Bitcoin)
    - Recent statement of any virtual currency you have, the amount and its current value
- Foreign Assets, trusts or bank accounts
    - Last 6 months of statements on all accounts
- Life Insurance
    - Statement showing the premium and cash value of life insurance
- Real Estate
    - Printouts for the value of any real estate owned (appraisal, Zillow, etc)
    - Recent mortgage statements for any property owned

- Recent statement for credit lines/home equity loans secured by any real estate
- Automobiles
    - Kelly Blue Book printouts for value of each vehicle
    - Recent monthly statement of any loan balance and monthly payment
    - Recent monthly statement showing the lease payment and time remaining on the lease
- Collectables (artwork, jewelry, collections, etc)
    - Statement of value or appraisal for collectables
    - Copy of your homeowners or renter's insurance including riders.

Income & Expenses:

- We need your current income for you and your spouse/partner/significant other you reside with/anyone who contributes to the household income (whether they are responsible or not). Please get us any of the following if they apply:
    - A current profit and loss for each business or rental activity
    - If you or your spouse are wage earners, your three most recent pay stubs
    - Proof of any social security income
    - Proof of annuity or retirement income
    - Proof of any child support or alimony received
    - Proof of any other income or cash flow stream into the household
- Last three months of utility bills
- Proof of your mortgage payment and balance. If you rent, we need your current lease agreement
- Proof of monthly car payments, whether loan or lease, with the balance remaining
- Proof of health insurance and premium amount
- Proof of life insurance premiums
- Proof of disability insurance premiums
- Proof of any alimony or child support you or your spouse pay, including the divorce or separation agreement and court order

- Home equity statement
- Proof of any judgments and payment plans to secured creditors
- Proof of any payment plans with state taxing authorities
- Proof of student loan balances and payments
- Proof of current estimated tax payments (unless you are a wage earner, in which case they are reflected on your paystubs)
- Proof of out-of-pocket healthcare expenses, IF they exceed $52/per person per month (or $114/month for anyone 65 or older)
- Proof of child/dependent care expense, such as daycare and after-school programs
- Proof of any other necessary expenses, such as mandatory union dues, restitution payments, etc.

Letter to RO – CNC Status 1

June 1, 2021

VIA FEDERAL EXPRESS
_____, Revenue Officer
Internal Revenue Service
STREET ADDRESS
CITY, STATE ZIP

    Re: **Taxpayer Names, SSNs**

Dear Ms. REVENUE OFFICER:

Pursuant to your request, enclosed please find the following documents:

1. Three months of bank account statements for all bank accounts;
2. An updated Form 433A executed by the taxpayers;
3. A copy of Mr. TAXPAYER's termination letter;
4. An updated life insurance statement; and
5. A recent auto repair bill for their vehicle.

Housing and Utilities

The taxpayers are presently living with family and trying to save for an apartment. Accordingly, $2,120/month was used as the housing expense, representing what the taxpayers are currently spending (cell phone, storage unit and other expenses) as well as the amount each month they are attempting to save in order to move out of their daughter's house.

Vehicle Operating Expense

The taxpayers share one car, which is now 9 years old. We have included an invoice for a necessary car repair to show the amount of money the car is costing the taxpayers on a regular basis. When last asked to respond regarding the vehicle operating expense on March 31, 2021, we were able to substantiate $918/month of actual vehicle operating expenses. Accordingly, we left the amount that was substantiated in our March 31, 2021 submission on Form 433A. In further support of this being a reoccurring expense, pursuant to the bank account statements, there was a November 26, 2021 expense of $1,189.8 for maintenance (paid to AUTO REPAIR) as well as gas, insurance and other expenses. The IRS recognizes that aged vehicles cost more to maintain, as they allow an extra $200/month when evaluating an offer-in-compromise.

Out-of-Pocket Health Care

The taxpayers' health is rapidly deteriorating. Mr. TAXPAYER has been diagnosed with moderate to severe centrilobular emphysema, Ramsey Hunt syndrome and bell's palsy. As of the drafting of this letter (1/13/2022), Mr. TAXPAYER is undergoing urgent testing at the hospital due to issues with his liver. Mrs. TAXPAYER is also under care of various specialists and takes prescription medicines. We have highlighted their medical expenses in the three months of bank statements that we provided. The expenses add up to $7,062 for the three-month period, or $2,354/month. Extensive medical backup was provided in our March 31, 2021 document submission. Their medical expenses are significant, and they do not have any supplement insurance plans (other than Medicare) to help pay for them.

Other Comments

Please note the balance in the bank account is prior to the taxpayers remitting their fourth quarter 2021 estimated tax payment (they had self-employment income in first quarter, prior to Mr. TAXPAYER's termination). You will also note Mr. TAXPAYER writes Mrs. TAXPAYER checks from his bank account so that Mrs. TAXPAYER can deposit it into their joint account to pay bills (we have included copies of these checks to verify this).

Request for Uncollectible Status

Given the taxpayers' age, poor financial condition, and deteriorating health, we respectfully request the IRS to place the taxpayers in uncollectible status since there is no viable alternative at this time.

Very truly yours,

TAX PRO NAME

Enclosures

C. TAXPAYER NAMES

Letter to RO – CNC Status 2 – Home Foreclosure

June 1, 2021

<u>VIA FEDERAL EXPRESS</u>
_____, Revenue Officer
Internal Revenue Service
STREET ADDRESS
CITY, STATE ZIP

   Re: Taxpayer Names, SSNs

Dear Ms. REVENUE OFFICER:

Enclosed please find Form 433A for the above-referenced taxpayers. There are exigent circumstances in this case, as Mr. TAXPAYER is extremely ill. He had a brain tumor removed and then suffered a major stroke from the operation. He is completely paralyzed on his left side of his body. He is undergoing therapy and can only travel via ambulette. Mrs. TAXPAYER suffers from mental illness and the sheer stress of her husband's ailments have not helped her situation.

They have two mortgages on their home (Cenlar and Chase). The Cenlar mortgage is currently in foreclosure. The Chase mortgage is currently being paid from the taxpayers' daughter's bank account as the taxpayers have no means to pay the mortgage. The daughter pays for most of their bills, such as their medical/medical related travel and other necessities. The taxpayers maintain no bank accounts.

The only income into the household is the income from Mrs. TAXPAYER's job as a salesperson at BUSINESS, a trinket shop in City. She makes roughly $2,000/month which barely covers the taxpayers' food and clothing expense. The expenses listed on the Form 433A are truly much higher, such as their housing and utilities, out of pocket medical and transportation. However, as you can see, they are very negative even with the IRS allowable expenses for each category. The taxpayers' daughter is helping support them.

The taxpayers have equity in their house, but with the foreclosure pending, they are unable to tap it. We respectfully request the taxpayers be placed in uncollectible status for a one-year period so they may, with the help of their daughter, get their house out of foreclosure and borrow from the equity in the house to pay their tax debt.

Please call with any questions.

Very truly yours,

TAX PRO NAME

Letter to RO – Make Company CNC

June 1, 2021

<u>VIA FAX: (866) 431-0277</u>
_____, Revenue Officer
Internal Revenue Service
STREET ADDRESS
CITY, STATE ZIP

   Re: **Company Name, Inc.**

Dear Ms. REVENUE OFFICER:

Pursuant to your request, we submit the enclosed Form 433B and supporting material. The accountant prepared the P&L for December 2020 through and including March 2021 (you will note that the P&Ls are broken out by month so that they will correlate to the bank statements). The accountant was unable to finish the months of April and May 2021—he is continuing to work as expeditiously as possible to finalize them (once they are ready, they will be forwarded to you).

Based on the financial information available for December through March, we believe the taxpayer should be placed in uncollectible status. In addition to the IRS debt, the business owes significant debts to the New York State Insurance Fund and to their general liability insurer, among other creditors. However, the taxpayer is continuing to reorganize and trim expenses where feasible. Therefore, their ability to repay their tax debt should be revisited within two (2) years for an increased ability to pay.

Please call with any questions.

Very truly yours,

TAX PRO NAME

Letter to ACS – Seasonal Painter

June 1, 2021

Internal Revenue Services
P.O. Box 8208
Philadelphia, PA 19101-8208

    Re: Taxpayer Names (SSNs)

Dear Sir or Madam:

Enclosed please find Form 433A and supporting documentation for the above-referenced taxpayers. Mr. TAXPAYER is the sole member of PAINTING Company, LLC. He has struggled financially for years.

During the fall and winter months, he is unable to get work. Business will pick up in the late spring and summer, especially as home-selling season begins. When he finally gets work, he is able to afford to pay some of his delinquent bills for his most vital living expenses. His wife, MRS TAXPAYER, recently became employed with the Town of _____ Board of Education and works approximately 16 hours a week.

Taxpayer inherited a 1/5 interest in property in Old Lyme, but cannot access any of the equity in said property because the other joint owners are unwilling to sell or mortgage the property. With respect to the cash value of Taxpayer's life insurance policy, Taxpayer is unable to access any equity as the surrender of its cash value would result in an ultimate policy lapse. Further, just to meet daily living expenses, Taxpayer has taken a $30,000 loan from his mother.

Given the taxpayers' precarious financial condition, we request that they be placed in uncollectable status. Please call with any questions.

Very truly yours,

TAX PRO NAME

Letter to Appeals – Request for CNC

June 1, 2021

<u>Via Fax: 866-217-8636</u>
Internal Revenue Service
Office of Appeals
SO NAME
Street Address
City, State Zip

      Re: Taxpayer Names (SSNs)

Dear Mr. SETTLEMENT OFFICER:

This office represents the taxpayers, TAXPAYER NAMES (collectively, the "Taxpayers" or "Mr. and Mrs. TAXPAYER"), before the Internal Revenue Service (the "IRS").

As set forth on the attached Form 433A, the Taxpayers are in a horrible financial situation. Mrs. TAXPAYER works in the court-reporting industry. Given the pandemic, she earned no income in 2020 because the courts were barely operating. Calendar year 2021 has been off to a very slow start because court operations are still backlogged; further, the business has not done any in-person depositions this year (remote only). It is unclear if the business will be able to attain pre-pandemic earnings or how long it may take for that to happen. Further, Mrs. TAXPAYER is 55 years old and suffers from health issues—she struggles to put in the long hours the business requires. Mr. TAXPAYER also suffers from significant health issues. The taxpayers' health issues are further detailed below.

By way of background, Mr. TAXPAYER' medical issues began in 2007 when he started experiencing significant back, neck and leg pain. Mr. TAXPAYER has undergone 8 major back surgeries, including multiple spinal fusions, as well as countless epidural injections and other various forms of treatment for his constant pain. His spine has been rebuilt two times. The medical records from the surgeries are attached hereto as **Exhibit A**. Mr. TAXPAYER continues to experience difficulty sleeping due to, at times, his unmanageable back pain; when he takes his prescribed muscle relaxers, it leaves him fatigued and unbalanced. Mr. TAXPAYER has experienced such extreme fatigue that there are several medically-documented instances of him falling, needing to work from home because he could no longer drive, no longer being able to work, and even rear ending someone because he fell asleep behind the wheel. Medical records illustrating these various issues are attached hereto as **Exhibit B**.

In further support of Mr. TAXPAYER' incapacity due to his medical issues, the Social Security Administration (the "SSA Decision") found that Mr. TAXPAYER was disabled from June 13, 2013 (the last day he was able to work) through the date of the decision, which was July 25, 2016. The SSA Decision is attached hereto as **Exhibit C**. The SSA Decision states, "[t]he medical evidence of record establishes the claimant has been fully compliant with numerous treatment modalities event after multiple back surgeries, including narcotic medications, rehabilitation and physical therapy; however, records from treating physician, Dr. NAME, establish the claimant has enjoyed no more than moderate pain relief from such treatment." In sum, Mr. TAXPAYER continues to suffer from immense, constant and long-term pain.

In addition to Mr. TAXPAYER' medical condition, Mrs. TAXPAYER has underwent a major surgery. Mrs. TAXPAYER had a high risk of breast cancer due to a genetic predisposition and underwent a double mastectomy in 2012. Mrs. TAXPAYER' medical records are attached hereto as Exhibit D. The stress of her struggling business and their overall insolvency due to their tax debt has also further depressed her mental state.

The taxpayers have two residences—a Connecticut home and a secondary home in South Carolina. Mr. TAXPAYER spends most of his time in South Carolina because the cold Connecticut weather further aggravates his back issues. On the other hand, Mrs. TAXPAYER spends much of her time in Connecticut. Her business primarily operates in Connecticut. Further, she needs to be close to her adult son, Dylan. Dylan suffers from post-concussion syndrome from being struck in the head. Both of their properties are in forbearance, as there has been no extra funds to pay the mortgages. The forbearance period ends in September 2021. For purposes of calculating their housing and utility expenses on Form 433A, the regular mortgage payments were used as this necessary expense will imminently resume.

As further evidence of the taxpayers' poor financial state, they have been borrowing on credit cards to pay their necessary expenses. This has left them in significant credit card debt. They are also in an installment agreement with the State of Connecticut for $750/month to repay their delinquent taxes. This payment is a necessary expense that should be allowed in full, as it was set up to prevent the imminent threat of levy action.

The Taxpayers had hoped to file an offer in compromise at this time, but are concerned about potential issues resulting from the IRS' pending review of their 2019 tax return. If there was any tax that the IRS determined was due, the Taxpayers would have no way of paying it and it would need to be included in their offer. Clearly, the Taxpayers have no way of repaying their tax obligations in full.

For the above reasons, we respectfully request that the Taxpayers be placed in currently not collectible status as there is no viable alternative at this time.

Please call with any questions.

Very truly yours,

TAX PRO NAME

C. TAXPAYERS

Letter for Release of Levy Due to Hardship

FEDEX

January ___, 20____

Revenue Officer A. Smith
Internal Revenue Service
Street Address
City, State Zip

Re: Levy on TAXPAYER'S NAME, SSN ****

Dear Ms. Smith,

We submitted the 433-A you requested along with all of the taxpayer's supporting documentation. As we discussed you agree with our conclusion that the Taxpayer has no ability to pay and should have their account placed in "Uncollectible" status. Despite this, however, you indicated that you had no intention of releasing the levy on the taxpayer's wages because of the taxpayer's missing 2019 return.

I wanted to point out that you are legally obligated to release the levy regardless of the taxpayer's compliance. Pursuant to IRC § 6343 a levy must be released if it is causing economic hardship, which is defined as someone who is "Uncollectible." The United States Tax Court has reiterated this in its decision in *Kathleen A. Vinatieri v. Commissioner, Docket No. 15895-08L (2009).*

In its decision, the United States Court stated:

> Under regulations prescribed by the Secretary, the Secretary must release a levy upon all, or part of, a taxpayer's property or rights to property if, inter alia, the Secretary has determined that the levy is creating an economic hardship due to the financial condition of the taxpayer. Sec. 6343(a)(1)(D), I.R.C. The regulations provide that a levy is creating an economic hardship due to the financial condition of an individual taxpayer and must be released "if satisfaction of the levy in whole or in part will cause an individual taxpayer to be unable to pay his or her reasonable basic living expenses." Sec. 301.6343-1(b)(4), Proced. & Admin. Regs.

Sec. 6343(a)(1)(D), I.R.C., and sec. 301.6343-1(b)(4), Proced. & Admin. Regs., require release of a levy that creates an economic hardship regardless of the taxpayer's noncompliance with filing required returns.

If you disagree, please respond in writing explaining your authority. Otherwise please release the levy and fax us a copy of the release. I will continue to work with the taxpayer to get the missing return completed and filed with you.

I can be reached at (xxx) xxx-xxxx if you wish to discuss this further.

Very truly yours,

YOUR NAME

Made in the USA
Middletown, DE
10 July 2025

10288007R00163